WHITEWATER COOKS

together again

Shelley Adams

Early on in my association with the *Whitewater Cooks* series, a buyer for a large national retail chain commented to me that she felt the Whitewater series was a "western phenomenon." Five cookbooks later, this phenomenon has captured the passion of home cooks across Canada and in the U.S. With over 250,000 copies sold, Shelley Adams has consistently inspired home cooks with her impressive and easy to make recipes. At a time when we all want to be together again, Shelley's new cookbook will be an essential and elegant culinary cornerstone in that journey.

NANCY WISE, Sandhill Book Marketing Ltd.

Published by **Alicon Holdings Ltd.** Nelson B.C.

ISBN 978-0-9811424-4-9

All photographs except as noted copyright © 2021 David R. Gluns. All rights reserved.
David Gluns by Glory Vitug, Claire Hitchman by Charlie Hitchman, Gillian Stead by Marin Hudson

Author: **Shelley Adams** · whitewatercooks.com
Photography: **David R. Gluns** · gluns.ca
Design and layout: **Gillian Stead**
Edited by: **Marlene Cornelis** · **Veranda Editorial**

❧ *We eat all the food photographed in our books!*

Distributed by **Sandhill Book Marketing,**
sandhillbooks.com · info@sandhillbooks.com

Distributed by **Independent Publishers Group (IPG)** · orders@ipgbook.com
Check out **whitewatercooks.com** to see where you can purchase the series.

Printed and bound in Canada by **Friesens Book Division**

This book is dedicated to everyone out there.
We've been through an unprecedented time
here on Earth — let's be together again!

4 x 21 (21)

WHITEWATER COOKS
together again

contents

Introduction

❧

BELIEVE IT OR NOT, I named this book *Together Again* before the pandemic began. I loved the idea of us all being together again on the pages of a new *Whitewater Cooks* cookbook. I could not have imagined that by the time this book was published, we still wouldn't have been able to cook or dine together in the comfort of our homes for such a long, long time.

I now see these recipes as a way to reinvigorate people's love and enthusiasm for food during this unprecedented time as we all discover what matters most — being together. With more time on our hands to plan and fine-tune our cooking skills, my hope is that these varied and delicious new recipes will be treasured in the way our feelings are when we're side-by-side at a boisterous and beautiful table. Here is a collection of recipes that you can try in your kitchens in anticipation of us all joining together again.

While creating this book, the return of my son, Conner, from New York City was the real silver lining in a COVID cloud. From April through August we invented and tested recipes, cooked and dined together. Conner is a talented and passionate chef and his love of cooking for a crowd shines through these pages! Like mother, like son?

My journey with this cookbook also had to navigate a few injuries that altered the book's trajectory. A broken wrist and fractured kneecap meant I had to postpone the photo shoots. The upside of this is that it gave me a chance to slow down and contemplate, research, and ultimately write *Together Again*. I love creating simple yet elegant recipes for the world to enjoy and, despite all the setbacks, this was a joyful time.

What started out as a cookbook to showcase my favourite recipes from the five previous books turned into cookbook number six, containing almost 80 amazing and brand-new recipes. It was Thanksgiving 2018 when my kids, Ali and Conner, said, "Mom, you still have tons of new recipes and ideas to share."

I am forever grateful for their infusion of ideas that include Korean- and Moroccan-influenced recipes alongside new twists on my trademark West Coast and Mediterranean-influenced fare … bringing us all together again!

Conner and Shelley Adams

Yuki Conne

Mike Adams and Lucy

Alexa Adams

Acknowledgements

✤

WITH ALL MY HEART, I would like to thank my small but mighty team who created *Together Again*. I appreciate their patience and resilience despite the particular challenges we faced, whether it was pandemic limitations or my injury-related delays.

Thank you so much to the amazing and very talented David Gluns for his stunning photography and artistic touch. We have such a connection and dedication to creating the *Whitewater Cooks* series together that I can't imagine working side-by-side with anyone else but David.

Thanks beyond measure to my son, Conner, for his background technical work and most of all for sharing so many delicious recipes, teaching me so much about new food trends and techniques, and keeping us current with the food that people are eating and making in New York City. Having him home and collaborating closely for four months was definitely a happy consequence of the pandemic.

To my brilliant daughter, Alexa, thanks for her constant support and frequent and well-thought-out feedback during the writing process. I also so greatly appreciated her sharp eye on the all-important cover choice.

Linda Klein, Sue McLaughlin, Sue Donaldson, Margie Rosling, Alivia McKenzie, Marie Weeks, Sheri Weichel, Beverly Grimshaw, Bernice Hetherington, Gail Morrison, Paul Morrison, Bailey Singer, Marcia Hetherington, Cal and Loree Renwick, and Duncan Carey.

To the artists whose creations add so much beauty to the pages of this book: Yuki Conne, Vincent Massey, Erin Prospero, Heinz Laffin, and Selena Sced, pottery; Walter Latin, wooden spoons; Glenn McCallum, wooden bowls; and Kyla Jakovitz, Bella Flora flowers. Being a lover of beauty and art and everything handmade, I thank them with all my heart!

To Yuki Conne, thanks not just for her beautiful pottery but for the constant support with this cookbook. I can't wait to meet her baby!

Thank you to Railway Specialty Meats and Delicatessen and to the Fisherman's Market for all their delicious treasures from both land and sea. Thanks also to Kristie Steele for her beautiful baking.

My immense thanks to Claire Hitchman and Mila Stasieczek for all their cooking and beautiful food styling to prepare for the perfect shots. We all put our heads together to create the gorgeous sets for each recipe.

To Nancy Wise, thanks for promoting and selling the *Whitewater Cooks* series with so much enthusiasm and dedication, and for her inspiring testimonial. We adore her.

Recipe testing is an intensive and substantial part of creating a cookbook — so much gratitude to Emmy McKnight and Claire Hitchman. I so cherish their attention to detail and opinions.

An enormous amount of gratitude to the family and friends who shared their recipes with me, making the cookbook so delicious and diverse. Thank you so much Conner Adams, Ali Adams, Mike Adams, Petra Lehmann, Blake Covernton, Mary Ellen McKnight, Claire Hitchman,

Mila Stasieczek | Claire Hitchman

The three of us laughed so much and worked so hard. We were a fine-tuned trio during the winter and spring while creating *Together Again,* and were even filmed for a sweet Nelson Kootenay Lake Tourism video during a photo shoot for this book. *Grazie bellas*! Thanks also to my ever-supportive and so cherished girlfriends.

Thank you so much for the sharp and focused brains of the initial proofreaders Mike Adams, Sarah Dobell, and Ross Hitchman. Also to Jane Byers for the fabulous testimonial that she contributed to this latest cookbook in the series. I am so honoured.

So much gratitude to editor Marlene Cornelis who went above and beyond her editing duties to help with recipe writing and streamlining, enhancing our readers' cooking and reading experience.

Bravo to Gillian Stead for once again taking our recipes and David's photos and designing a masterpiece. Gill is beyond patient and a consummate professional. We are so fortunate to have her design this book.

To my husband Mike and our dog Lucy, thank you for being so darn loyal and cute!

I love you all!

starters

Grilled Scallops
with Nori Flakes and Wasabi Lime Sauce · 18

Tomato and Olive **Tarte Tatin** · 20

Chinese Five-Spice **Szechuan Peanuts** · 22

Roasted Beet and Walnut Dip
with Greek Yogurt and Za'atar · 23

Marinated Manchego Cheese
and Castelvetrano Olives · 24

Sharp Cheddar, Smoked Ham and Apple **Galette** · 26

Shrimp Cocktail
with Lemon Basil Aioli and Spicy Cocktail Sauce · 28

Chili Con Queso Dip with Pico de Gallo · 30

Lovely's Rustic Boulangerie **Bread** · 32

Crab Summer Rolls
with Curry Peanut and Nuoc Cham Sauce · 34

Three **Toasts** · 36

Burrata
with Chimichurri Sauce and Harissa Roasted Tomatoes · 38

Spicy Lamb Meatballs
with Mint Pesto and Greek Yogurt · 40

Blake's **Ceviche** · 42

Grilled Scallops
with Nori Flakes and Wasabi Lime Sauce

These scallops make a nice light starter to any dinner. They're flavourful and easy to prepare, which is always a good thing!
SERVES 4

ingredients

1 cup mayonnaise
½ lime, juice
½ tsp wasabi paste
½ tsp kosher or sea salt
1 toasted nori sheet
1 tsp ground coriander
½ tsp ground ginger
2 tbsp vegetable oil,
  plus more for grill
16 large sea scallops
½ lime, zest
  (reserve lime half)
3 green onions, dark green
  parts only, very thinly sliced
1 tsp red pepper flakes

method

Soak 4 8-inch wooden skewers in water for 15 minutes
to prevent them from catching on fire when grilled.

Mix mayonnaise, lime juice, wasabi, salt and 1 tbsp water
in a small bowl and set aside.

Grind nori into fine flakes in a spice mill or food processor.

Transfer to a small bowl and set aside for serving.

Combine coriander, ginger and vegetable oil in a large bowl.

Pat the scallops dry with paper towels.

Add scallops to the oil mixture and toss to coat.

Place 4 scallops onto each skewer.

Season both sides with salt.

Heat barbecue to medium-high heat (about 375°F).

Barbecue scallops until grill marks appear and the scallops are just
cooked through, about 3 minutes per side. If you don't have a barbecue,
use a cast-iron grill pan and cook for 3 minutes per side.

Spread wasabi lime sauce on individual serving plates
and place a skewer of scallops on top.

Sprinkle with lime zest and a squeeze of lime juice.

Garnish with green onions, red pepper flakes and ground nori.

*These lovely skewers of grilled scallops also make a beautiful lunch
paired with our Edamame Rice Noodle Salad (page 64).*

starters

Tomato and Olive
Tarte Tatin

My son, Conner, was home for the first four and a half months of the pandemic and he cooked us so many delicious things! One day he said, "I have a little tomato treat for you guys before dinner tonight." It was the most beautiful and delicious tomato and olive tarte made with flaky puff pastry in the tatin style. We loved it, and you will too. SERVES 4

ingredients

1 14-oz package puff pastry
2 tbsp unsalted butter
3 medium red onions,
   halved and thinly sliced
¼ cup plus 1 pinch sugar,
   divided
1 tbsp balsamic
   or red wine vinegar
⅓ cup pitted Kalamata olives,
   whole
1½ pints red and yellow
   cherry or grape tomatoes
   (3 cups)
1 tbsp fresh thyme
   or oregano leaves,
   plus sprigs for garnish
salt and pepper to taste
½ cup goat cheese,
   crumbled

You could also make this tarte earlier and eat it at room temperature. Adding goat cheese to the top of the warm tarte is absolutely divine!

method

Preheat oven to 425°F.

Thaw pastry until still cold, but not frozen.

(You can take it out of the freezer the day before and leave it in the fridge.)

Unfold pastry and roll into a 10-inch round, using the pan you will bake the tarte in as a template.

Put in the fridge until ready to use.

Melt butter in a large skillet over medium heat.

Add onions and pinch of sugar and cook, stirring until the onions are golden and caramelized, about 15–20 minutes.

Add 2 tbsp water and let it cook down, scraping brown bits from the bottom of the pan.

Transfer onions to a bowl and set aside.

Combine ¼ cup sugar and 3 tbsp water in an ovenproof 9-inch skillet or cast-iron pan.

Cook over medium heat, swirling gently but not stirring, until sugar melts and turns amber in colour and smells caramelized, 5–10 minutes.

Add the vinegar, being mindful of splattering, and swirl gently. Turn off heat.

Arrange olives over the caramel, then top with the tomatoes and onions.

Sprinkle with the thyme or oregano leaves and season with salt and pepper.

Top with the chilled puff pastry round, tucking the edges down inside the pan.

Cut several long slits in the top of the pastry.

Bake tarte until the crust is puffed and golden, about 30 minutes.

Let tarte rest for 5 minutes, then run a knife around the pastry edge to loosen it from the pan.

Invert tarte onto a wire rack and let rest for 5–10 minutes before scattering goat cheese on top and serving on your prettiest platter.

Slice and devour!

Chinese Five-Spice
Szechuan Peanuts

These sweet, salty, fiery and crunchy peanuts are hard to stop eating, especially with beer!

8-10 SERVINGS

ingredients

2   cups raw peanuts, blanched
    vegetable oil for frying peanuts
8   red Chinese or Thai chili
    peppers, 4 left whole and
    4 with seeds removed and
    cut into thin strips
1   tsp whole Szechuan peppercorns
1   tsp sugar
2   tsp salt
1   tsp Szechuan peppercorns,
    ground
1   tsp Chinese five-spice

method

Arrange peanuts on a baking sheet and freeze for at least 2 hours. This will dehydrate the nuts so they crisp up faster when fried.

Place frozen peanuts in a wok or medium pot and pour in oil to cover by ¼ inch.

Bring to a simmer over medium heat and cook until peanuts are golden brown, about 15–20 minutes.

Remove peanuts from oil using a spider or slotted spoon and transfer to drain on paper towels.

Discard all but 1 tsp of the oil.

Add sliced chili peppers, whole chili peppers and whole Szechuan peppercorns to the skillet with remaining oil.

Stir constantly over medium-high heat until fragrant, about 2 minutes. (Don't let the chilies brown; you want them to stay red.)

Mix in peanuts, sugar, salt, ground Szechuan peppercorns and Chinese five-spice.

Transfer to a bowl and let cool.

These yummy peanuts can be stored in an airtight container for up to 2 weeks.

Roasted Beet and Walnut Dip
with Greek Yogurt and Za'atar

If you're tired of dips made with hummus and mayonnaise, make this vibrant pink dip for a healthy change and beautiful presentation. Serve with homemade pita chips and crudités for a perfect little snack before dinner or on the boat before a swim in Queens Bay. SERVES 4-6

ingredients

1   lb beets (about
    3-4 medium beets)
½ cup walnuts, toasted
    and finely chopped
2   tbsp fresh dill, chopped,
    plus sprigs for serving
2   tbsp full-fat Greek yogurt
    or sour cream,
    plus 1 tbsp for garnishing
1   tsp balsamic vinegar
1   tsp sea salt
½ tsp freshly ground black pepper
1   tsp za'atar (a Middle Eastern
    spice blend)
2   tbsp extra virgin olive oil
    for serving

method

Preheat oven to 375°F.

Place unpeeled beets in an ovenproof baking dish and add water to cover beets ⅓ of the way up.

Cover with tin foil and roast for about 40 minutes or until soft when poked with a skewer.

Remove from oven and peel with a paring knife or vegetable peeler, then coarsely chop.

Place beets, walnuts, dill, yogurt or sour cream, vinegar, salt and pepper in food processor and blend until smooth.

Spoon into a pretty serving bowl and top with remaining yogurt or sour cream, the za'atar, dill sprigs and a drizzle of olive oil.

*Za'atar is an ancient and iconic spice blend enjoyed across the Middle East.
It can be sprinkled on virtually everything like flatbreads, hummus, dips, vegetables and rice. You can
also make this dip with roasted carrots and serve both beet and carrot dips for extra colour and beauty!*

Marinated Manchego Cheese
and Castelvetrano Olives

Marinated cheese is such a yummy treat and so easy to whip together to have on hand for unexpected aperitif-hour guests! It keeps in the fridge for days and is best eaten at room temperature. Pair it with your favourite crackers or baguette. If cantaloupe is in season, wrap some slices with prosciutto and serve with this flavourful marinated Manchego for a gorgeous appetizer. SERVES 4

ingredients

1   cup olive oil
1   head garlic
    (about 12 cloves),
    separated and peeled
1   lemon, quartered through
    stem end, thinly sliced
    crosswise, seeds removed
2   sprigs rosemary
4   sprigs thyme
1   cup Castelvetrano or
    Cerignola olives, pitted
1   tsp sea salt
¼   tsp black pepper
½   tsp red chili flakes
½   lb Manchego cheese
    (youngest you can find),
    cut or broken into
    ¾-inch pieces

method

Heat olive oil, garlic and lemon in a small saucepan over medium heat, stirring occasionally, until garlic starts to turn golden, 15–20 minutes.

Remove from heat, add rosemary and thyme sprigs and olives.

Season with salt, pepper and red chili flakes. Let cool.

Pour garlic mixture into a medium-size bowl, add cheese and stir to coat.

Cover and chill for at least 12 hours before serving.

You can also use Gouda, Monterey Jack or white cheddar cheese if you can't find Manchego. A blood orange is also a lovely option instead of the lemon.

Sharp Cheddar, Smoked Ham and Apple
Galette

My dentist has the best waiting room, with really good gourmet cooking and interior design magazines, yummy teas and cosy furniture. It's a great way to take your mind off one of life's necessary outings. I was so excited when I saw a photo of this savoury galette there one day. It makes a lovely starter or a beautiful lunch served with a little frisée or spring greens salad! SERVES 4–6

ingredients

Cornmeal Dough

This makes enough dough for two galettes. You can freeze one disc for later use.

¼ cup sour cream
¼ cup ice water
1 cup flour
⅓ cup cornmeal
½ tsp salt
½ cup cold butter, cut into cubes

Filling

1 tbsp salted butter
2 tbsp all-purpose flour
¾ cup milk
2 tbsp grainy mustard
½ tsp nutmeg
2 cups aged cheddar cheese, grated
250 g smoked ham, thinly sliced
2 baking apples, cored and sliced
   into ⅛-inch slices (peels left on)
1 tsp lemon zest
leaves of 2 thyme branches
salt and pepper

method

Cornmeal Dough

Stir the sour cream and ice water together in a small bowl.

Put the flour, cornmeal and salt in a mixing bowl and stir with a whisk until combined.

Add the cold butter and work it with your fingers or a pastry blender until you have a nice, crumbly mixture.

Add the sour cream mixture all at once to the dry ingredients with a wooden spoon and mix until it forms a loose ball.

Shape into 2 flat discs. Use some flour on your fingers to keep it from sticking.

Wrap in plastic wrap and place in the fridge for at least 2 hours.

Filling

Preheat oven to 375°F.

Melt the butter in a small heavy-bottomed saucepan over medium heat.

Add the flour and whisk until incorporated.

Whisk in the milk gradually. When the sauce is smooth and starting to thicken, add the mustard, nutmeg and cheese and continue stirring until the sauce is thick and smooth.

Remove from heat.

to assemble

Roll the dough out on a floured surface, into a circle about 11 inches in diameter.

Spread the cheese sauce on the middle of the dough, leaving about 2 inches around the edge.

Place the ham slices on the sauce.

Arrange the apples on top, allowing some of the ham to show through.

Top with lemon zest and thyme leaves.

Sprinkle with salt and pepper.

Fold the edges of the dough rustically to form the galettes.

Press gently to hold the edges together a bit.

Bake for 40–45 minutes.

Remove from the oven and let rest for 10–15 minutes before slicing.

We use the same cornmeal dough for this as for the Rustic Tomato Tarts found in Whitewater Cooks at Home *and the Little Individual Rustic Fruit Tarts found in this book (page 168). This cornmeal dough is so versatile. I usually make a double batch and keep a few discs in the freezer.*

Shrimp Cocktail
with Lemon Basil Aioli and Spicy Cocktail Sauce

Everyone loves a good shrimp cocktail even if they won't admit it! It's the first thing to be devoured by kids, teenagers and adults alike at any party or picnic. Every year we'd have to tell our kids not to eat too many of the prawns at our friends the Diamonds' Christmas Eve party. I like the combo of this hot and spicy classic cocktail sauce and the mild, creamy, lemony one. SERVES 6–8

ingredients

Shrimp
2–3 pounds large raw shrimp, unpeeled
salt for the poaching water
1   large onion, quartered
¼   cup black peppercorns
3   lemons (2 in wedges for garnishing,
     1 for squeezing on prawns)
½   cup fresh parsley leaves

Cocktail Sauce
1   cup ketchup
½   lemon, juice
1   tbsp harissa paste
2   tsp Worcestershire sauce
½   tsp salt
½   tsp pepper
1   tsp horseradish

Lemon Basil Aioli Sauce
2   large egg yolks, room temperature
2   tsp fresh lemon juice
½   tsp salt
½   cup olive oil
½   cup vegetable oil
1   small garlic clove, finely grated
1   tsp fresh lemon juice
1   tbsp lemon zest
½   cup basil leaves, thinly sliced

method

Shrimp
Peel the shrimp, leaving tails on.
Bring a large pot of highly salted water to a boil and add the onion and peppercorns.
Lower the shrimp into the water in batches and cook just until bright pink and opaque, 3–4 minutes.
Remove cooked shrimp with a slotted spoon and transfer to a baking sheet so they can cool down as quickly as possible.
Put them in the fridge to cool if you have room.

Cocktail Sauce
Combine the cocktail sauce ingredients in a medium-size bowl and set aside.

Lemon Basil Aioli Sauce
Whisk the egg yolks, lemon juice and the salt together in a food processor or medium-size bowl.
Combine both oils in a measuring cup with a spout.
Add oil to the egg mixture in a slow steady stream, one tablespoon at a time, whisking to ensure the oil is completely incorporated before adding another tablespoon.
Whisk in garlic, lemon juice and lemon zest.
Stir in basil.
Set aside.

to serve

Squeeze the fresh lemon over the cooled shrimp.
Fill a large bowl or serving platter with ice.
Put some of the cocktail sauce into the bottom of your favourite little serving dishes.
Hang shrimp around the edge of each dish and nestle the dishes into the ice.
Serve both sauces on the side.
Scatter the lemon wedges and parsley on top of the ice.

You will probably have leftover cocktail sauce, which is always a good thing. It will keep for up to 2 weeks in the fridge.

Chili con Queso Dip
with Pico de Gallo

If you need to make a big, cheesy, filling snack for watching the Grey Cup or Super Bowl or to feed a group of hungry skiers, this is a good one! It's also a great dish to take to the cabin.   SERVES 6 OR MORE

ingredients

Meat Layer
1 tbsp vegetable oil
1 lb lean ground beef
½ medium onion, diced
½ green pepper, diced
2 garlic cloves, minced
1 tsp salt
½ tsp pepper
2 tsp ground cumin
2 tsp chili powder
1 cup beef or chicken stock

Cheesy Layer
3 tbsp butter
½ medium onion, finely diced
1 large poblano chili,
   seeded and finely diced
2–3 jalapeno peppers seeded
   and finely diced, about 2 tbsp
2 garlic cloves, minced
2 medium tomatoes, diced
3 tsp chipotle peppers
   in adobo sauce, finely diced
1 tsp salt
2 tbsp flour
1½ cups milk
2 cups Monterey Jack cheese,
   grated
2 cups aged cheddar cheese,
   grated

Pico de Gallo
6 Roma tomatoes, finely diced
¼ white onion, finely diced
1–2 jalapeno peppers,
   seeded and finely diced,
   about 2 tsp
1 lime, juice
½ cup cilantro, chopped
½ tsp salt
¼ tsp pepper

For Serving
1 cup sour cream
1 cup guacamole (optional)
cilantro sprigs
2 green onions, chopped

method

Meat Layer

Heat oil in a large skillet over medium-high heat and add beef. Break up and stir until browned but not cooked through (6–8 minutes).

Transfer to a bowl, leaving the most fat possible in the pan.

Lower heat to medium. Sauté onion, pepper and garlic, stirring until soft but not brown, 6–8 minutes. Season with salt and pepper.

Add cumin and chili powder. Cook a minute until spices are fragrant.

Add stock and reserved beef plus accumulated juices and bring to a simmer. Cook until liquid has evaporated, about 8–10 minutes.

Cover until ready to use or refrigerate until the next day.

Pico de Gallo

Mix all pico de gallo ingredients.

Refrigerate until ready to serve. (Can be made a day ahead.)

Cheesy Layer

Melt butter in a heavy-bottomed saucepan over medium heat.

Sauté onion, chili, jalapenos and garlic, stirring until soft but not browned, 8–10 minutes.

Add tomatoes, chipotle and salt.

Cook until juices have evaporated, about 6 minutes.

Stir in flour and cook until incorporated, about 1 minute.

Whisk in milk and cook until mixture comes to a boil and thickens, about 4 minutes.

Reduce heat to low. Gradually add cheeses, stirring constantly until cheese is completely melted and the sauce is smooth. (Can be made a day ahead and refrigerated.)

to assemble

Reheat the meat and cheese layers separately if made the day before.

Spread the warm meat layer in a 2-quart baking dish and pour the warm cheesy sauce over top. Broil briefly.

Top with a big scoop of pico de gallo, then sour cream, guacamole, cilantro sprigs, and chopped green onions.

Serve with homemade or store-bought tortilla chips.

Boulangerie Bread

My two friends Linda and Claire, a.k.a. Lovely and Clairence, are the best bread makers and bakers I know! This recipe is a combination of their two easy bread recipes made in a Dutch oven. It's hard to believe that a dough that requires absolutely no kneading produces such a beautiful loaf of bread! MAKES 1 LOAF

ingredients

2¾ cups all-purpose flour
¼ cup dark rye flour
2 tsp salt
¼ tsp instant yeast
1½ cups warm water
a handful of your favourite
    seeds (optional)

method

Combine flours, salt and yeast in a large bowl.

Add the water and mix together with your fingers or a wooden spoon to get a sticky and shaggy dough. (It takes less than a minute!)

Cover with plastic wrap and place in a warm part of the kitchen overnight or for a minimum of 6 hours.

Remove the dough from the bowl, place it on a lightly floured clean tea towel and turn the dough over and tuck in the edges to make a round loaf shape. Do not knead it.

Cover the dough with the other end of the tea towel or a new one and let it rest for another 2 hours.

Place a medium-size Dutch oven into the oven and preheat to 450°F.

Remove the Dutch oven once the oven has reached temperature and set it on a heatproof surface.

Sprinkle the dough with a handful of your favourite seeds if desired, dust it with a little flour and carefully set the dough seed-side-up into the hot Dutch oven. Then place back in the oven and bake for 30 minutes with the lid on and another 20 minutes with the lid off.

Remove from the oven, take the bread out and let cool on a baking rack for at least an hour.

This is a very versatile dough. You can add a handful of your favourite grains or seeds (like flaxseed, sunflower seeds, or pumpkin seeds) or even some olives and fresh herbs into the dough at the start of the mixing process. Once you start making this easy bread on a regular basis the process becomes second nature and the possibilities are endless!

You can make this bread in the morning and have it ready for your charcuterie board or dinner later in the day. Just make sure you let it rest for an hour before cutting.

Crab Summer Rolls
with Curry Peanut and Nuoc Cham Sauce

These beautiful and popular summer rolls originated in Hanoi. Here, they are often mislabelled as spring rolls. But spring rolls are deep fried and these light and fresh summer rolls are definitely not! The rice wraps are so delicate and the ingredients so fresh and light that the two sauces make for an over-the-top trio. I often like two different dipping sauces with things, a light clear one and a rich deep one, because why not? SERVES 4–6

ingredients

Curry Peanut Sauce

1 tbsp olive oil
½ cup red or green curry paste (or less if you don't like things very spicy)
1 14-oz can coconut milk
½ cup smooth peanut butter
3 tbsp rice vinegar
1 tbsp honey
salt and pepper

Nuoc Cham Sauce

1 lime, juice (about ¼ cup)
3 tbsp fish sauce
3 tbsp sugar
2 tbsp water
½ red Thai chili, seeded and finely diced (or ½ tsp red pepper flakes)
1 green onion, finely chopped
2 tsp fresh cilantro, finely chopped
2 tsp fresh mint, finely chopped

Summer Rolls

4 oz vermicelli rice noodles
¼–½ lb Dungeness crab meat, shredded
½ English cucumber, halved lengthwise, seeded and julienned
2 cups mint leaves
2 cups cilantro leaves
½ cup peanuts, roasted and finely chopped
4 green onions, trimmed to 10 inches and halved lengthwise
8 8-inch round rice paper wrappers

method

Curry Peanut Sauce

Heat oil over medium heat in a small saucepan.

Add red or green curry paste and cook in oil for 2–3 minutes.

Add coconut milk. Whisk out any small chunks and bring to a low simmer for 3–5 minutes.

Whisk in peanut butter, vinegar and honey and season to taste with salt and pepper.

Remove from heat and let cool until sauce starts to thicken.

Transfer to a small bowl for dipping.

Nuoc Cham Sauce

Combine all nuoc cham ingredients together in a small bowl and mix well.

Summer Rolls

Place rice noodles in a medium-size bowl and cover with boiling water. Let stand until softened, about 20 minutes.

Drain and rinse with cold water.

Place cooled noodles on a clean tea towel.

Prepare all summer roll ingredients and place on a platter or cutting board to be ready for assembly.

Fill a large shallow bowl with warm water.

Soak one rice paper wrapper in the water until just pliable, about 10 seconds.

Place on work surface and top wrapper with some of the crab, rice noodles, cucumber, mint, cilantro and peanuts.

Fold the wrapper tightly over the filling, tuck in the sides and roll up halfway.

Lay a green onion on top of the filling with 1 inch of overhang on one side and finish rolling.

Transfer to a platter and cover with a damp paper towel.

Repeat with the remaining wrappers and fillings.

Serve the rolls with the curry peanut and nuoc cham sauces.

These rolls can be covered with a damp paper towel and refrigerated for up to 1 hour. You could also use tofu, prawns or chicken in the filling, which would be equally delicious! A fresh, thinly-sliced mango would also be delish if you can find one.

starters

Three
Toasts

These three crostini toasts are the perfect combination for starting a dinner party. The inspiration for the ricotta and blue cheese toasts came from two restaurants in New York. The anchovy tomato toast is one my son, Conner, makes all the time because he loves anchovies so much! SERVES 6–8

ingredients

The Toasts
1 baguette (makes approximately 30 toasts)
½ cup olive oil
1 garlic clove, cut in half

Ricotta Toast
1 cup ricotta cheese
1 lemon, zest, or 1 preserved lemon, skin only, finely diced (recipe on page 86)
1 tsp freshly ground black pepper
2 mini cucumbers, thinly sliced
4 radishes, thinly sliced
1 package microgreens
Maldon salt and freshly ground black pepper for garnishing

Blue Cheese Toast
4 oz unsalted butter, room temperature
8 oz blue cheese, sliced
1 cup celery, sliced diagonally as thinly as possible
2 green onions or chives, sliced diagonally as thinly as possible
2 tbsp parsley, finely chopped
2 tbsp olive oil
1 lemon, juice
1 tsp sea salt
½ cup walnuts, roughly chopped
½ tsp pepper

Anchovy Toast
4 Roma tomatoes, finely diced or thinly sliced
1 50 g tin of anchovy fillets, sliced down the middle
⅓ cup flat-leaf parsley, coarsely chopped
1 tsp Maldon salt
1 tbsp red pepper flakes
2 tbsp olive oil for drizzling

method

The Toasts
Preheat oven to broil.
Slice a baguette into ½-inch slices on the diagonal or into rounds.
Place slices on a parchment-lined baking sheet.
Brush slices generously with olive oil on both sides.
Broil for 1 minute on each side, watching like a hawk that they don't burn!
Remove from oven and rub one side of each slice with a halved garlic clove.

Ricotta Toast
Whip together the ricotta, lemon zest or preserved lemon and pepper.
Spread ricotta thickly on toasts.
Top with cucumber and radish slices and microgreens.
Sprinkle with Maldon salt and freshly ground black pepper.

Blue Cheese Toast
Spread unsalted butter on each toast.
Add a layer of blue cheese.
Toss the celery with the green onions, parsley, olive oil, lemon juice and salt.
Pile the tossed celery and walnuts on each toast and top with a few grinds of black pepper.

Anchovy Toast
Place diced or sliced tomatoes on each toast and top with 2 sliced anchovy fillets.
Scatter flat-leaf parsley over top.
Sprinkle each toast with a pinch each of Maldon salt and red pepper flakes.
Drizzle olive oil over each toast.

It's fun to have all three kinds of toast at once, but having just one is still fabulous!

Burrata
with Chimichurri Sauce and Harissa Roasted Tomatoes

We had this starter in New York last spring and just loved it.
Burrata is such a treat and pairs well with so many things. This combo was a winner! SERVES 4

ingredients

1 large ball burrata cheese (250 g)
8–10 asparagus spears, steamed lightly and cooled, cut into 1-inch diagonal slices
½ cup hazelnuts, toasted and coarsely chopped

Crostini

1 baguette, sliced ½-inch thick
½ cup olive oil
1 garlic clove, cut in half

Chimichurri Sauce

¾ cup olive oil
3 tbsp red wine vinegar
1 lemon, juice
3 garlic cloves, peeled
3 shallots, peeled
1 tsp salt
½ tsp pepper
½ tsp red chili flakes
3 cups parsley, stems removed
2 cups cilantro, stems removed
1 cup fresh mint, stems removed

Roasted Cherry Tomatoes

2 tbsp olive oil
1 tbsp harissa paste
2 cups acorn or cherry tomatoes

method

Crostini

Preheat broiler.
Place baguette slices on a parchment lined baking sheet and brush liberally with olive oil on both sides.
Toast under broiler for 1 minute per side, watching carefully that they don't burn.
Remove from the oven and rub one side of each with the halved garlic clove.

Chimichurri Sauce — Makes about 4 cups.

Place olive oil, vinegar, lemon juice, garlic, shallots, salt, pepper and chili flakes in a food processor and pulse until chopped and well blended.
Add herbs by the handful and process until smooth.
Store in a mason jar in the fridge, as you will probably have some left.

Roasted Cherry Tomatoes

Preheat oven to 325°F.
Combine olive oil and harissa paste and toss with the tomatoes.
Place tomatoes on a baking sheet and roast for 30–35 minutes.

to serve

Spread about 2 cups of chimichurri sauce on a serving platter.
Set burrata ball in the middle.
Surround it with steamed asparagus and roasted tomatoes.
Scatter with toasted hazelnuts.
Drizzle burrata with some oil from roasting the tomatoes.
Serve with crostini.

Chimichurri is also great with any kind of barbecued meat or fish.
Feel free to use different fresh herbs — they all work beautifully in this fresh green sauce!
You can also peel some asparagus for a pretty presentation and texture.

Spicy Lamb Meatballs
with Mint Pesto and Greek Yogurt

I was in the airport on my way to Corsica when I saw a photo on the back of a magazine of these little treasures with a beautiful green mint pesto. I didn't have time to buy a copy, but kept remembering the picture and how badly I wanted to eat these meatballs. Here they are! SERVES 4

ingredients

Spicy Lamb Meatballs

1 large egg
½ cup panko
   (Japanese bread crumbs)
½ tsp ground cumin
¼ tsp crushed
   red pepper flakes
¼ tsp ground turmeric
¼ cup parsley, finely chopped
2 tbsp olive oil
1½ tsp sea salt
1 garlic clove, minced
1 lb ground lamb

Pesto

2½ cups mint leaves
2 cups parsley leaves
   with stems
3½ tbsp golden raisins
2 garlic cloves, minced
   (about 1½ tsp)
¾ cup olive oil
1 tsp salt

For Serving

1 cup Greek yogurt

method

Spicy Lamb Meatballs

Preheat oven to 450°F.

Position rack in upper third of the oven.

Combine egg, panko, cumin, red pepper flakes, turmeric, parsley, olive oil, salt and garlic in a large bowl.

Add lamb and mix with your hands until well combined.

Roll lamb mixture gently into 1½-inch diameter balls (about the size of a golf ball). Makes approximately 18 balls.

Place evenly apart on a parchment-covered baking sheet.

Bake meatballs until browned and cooked through, 12–15 minutes.

Pesto

Purée mint, parsley leaves and stems, raisins, garlic, ½ cup oil and salt in a blender or food processor until smooth.

to serve

Spread a thin layer of yogurt over plates, drizzle with pesto, place meatballs on top and drizzle on the remaining oil.

Something about the combination of raisins and mint in this pesto, paired with the flavourful lamb, really does it for me. Anything that has reminded me of far-away places in this past year is extra inviting!

Blake's
Ceviche

Blake is my friend who loves fish more than anyone in the world — seriously!
This is his fabulous recipe for ceviche. Feel free to divide the recipe in half if you don't have a big crowd to share it with.
SERVES 6-8

ingredients

1 red pepper, finely diced
1 yellow pepper, finely diced
1 white sweet onion, finely diced
3 large jalapeno peppers, seeded and finely diced
2 cloves garlic, minced
1 lb large scallops, cut into quarters
1 lb halibut fillet,
   skin off and cut into large bite-size pieces
1 lb medium-size prawns,
   peeled and chopped into bite-size pieces
4–6 limes, juice (1 cup fresh-squeezed lime juice)
1 cup olive oil
2 tbsp red wine vinegar
1 tbsp red Tabasco or sriracha hot sauce
2 tsp Maldon salt
¼ cup cilantro, roughly chopped
¼ cup flat leaf parsley, roughly chopped

method

Place all ingredients except the cilantro and parsley in a glass container with a tight-fitting lid.

Place in the fridge and let cure for 12 hours before serving.

Turn the container over several times or stir gently to blend flavours.

Remove from the fridge and place ceviche in a serving dish.

Stir in the cilantro and parsley.

Serve with homemade tortilla chips and cold beer or Pinot Grigio!

salads

Spicy Greens
with Goat Cheese Toasts, Apples and Poppy Seed Vinaigrette · 46

Fattoush Salad with Za'atar Dressing · 48

Heirloom Carrot **Salad** · 50

Petra's
Preserved Lemon and Crystallized Ginger Salad · 52

Chinese Five-Spice Salad
with Smashed Raspberries and Mangoes · 54

Yuzu **Summer Bowl** · 56

Butter Lettuce Salad
with Pickled Radishes and Creamy Feta Dill Dressing · 58

Spiced Lentil **Salade Niçoise** · 60

Honey Mustard **Brussels Sprouts Slaw** · 62

Kale and Cucumber Salad
with Roasted Ginger Dressing · 63

Edamame Rice Noodle Salad
with Tamarind Dressing · 64

Warm Roasted Potato Salad
with Wilted Kale and Creamy Tahini Dressing · 66

Frisée, Radicchio and Endive Salad
with Blue Cheese and Honey Walnuts · 68

Spicy Greens

with Goat Cheese Toasts, Apples and Poppy Seed Vinaigrette

With so many delicious varieties of apples available, it's hard to pick just one for this salad, so feel free to use a few. Honeycrisp, Pink Lady and GoldRush apples are some of my faves. Poppy seeds and honey are so yummy with the apples and the warm goat cheese toasts make for an amazing treat. Find the bitterest greens to balance all these flavours perfectly. SERVES 4

ingredients

Poppy Seed Vinaigrette

2 tbsp honey
3 tbsp apple cider vinegar
1 shallot, finely diced
1 tsp grainy or Dijon mustard
½ cup walnut oil
salt and pepper
2 tbsp poppy seeds

Goat Cheese Toasts

8 slices baguette, ½-inch thick
2 tbsp olive oil
salt and pepper
4 oz (113 g) soft goat cheese

Salad

2–3 apples
    (different varieties are nice)
½ lemon, juice
½ cup hazelnuts, roughly
    chopped and toasted
6–8 cups mixed bitter greens
    (endive, radicchio, arugula,
    mustard greens, mizuna),
    washed and dried

method

Poppy Seed Vinaigrette

Whisk together honey, vinegar, shallot and mustard in a small mixing bowl.

Drizzle in walnut oil, whisking slowly until emulsified.

Taste and season with salt and pepper.

Whisk in poppy seeds.

Goat Cheese Toasts

Preheat oven to 400°F.

Brush baguette slices with olive oil on both sides. Sprinkle with salt and pepper.

Brown in the oven until lightly toasted, flipping after about 3 minutes.

Set aside until needed.

Spread goat cheese on toast and set in a warm oven right before serving the salad.

Salad

Core apples and slice into thick matchsticks. Toss with lemon juice to prevent browning.

Toss apples and hazelnuts with a small amount of the Poppy Seed Vinaigrette.

Toss greens with enough of the dressing to lightly coat.

to serve

Place greens on serving plates and top with apple and hazelnut mixture.

Arrange goat cheese toasts over top or on the side.

Drizzle with a bit more olive oil.

This salad reminds me of something I loved eating in little bistros in France, and that's always a good memory to have! Top the goat cheese toasts with chopped fresh chives if you have some in your garden.

Fattoush Salad
with Za'atar Dressing

We adore this crunchy and flavourful Middle Eastern salad. Restaurants that serve Lebanese food often present it with a side of labneh and kalamata olives. In peach season, substitute some fresh peach slices for the tomatoes — it's absolutely amazing! SERVES 4

ingredients

Za'atar Dressing

2 tbsp sesame seeds, toasted
2 medium cloves garlic, minced
1 lemon, zest
1 tsp red chili flakes
1 tbsp dried oregano
1 tsp fresh thyme leaves
1 tsp sumac
½ tsp Maldon salt
1 lemon, juice
½ cup olive oil

Salad

2 pitas, torn into bite-size pieces
3 tbsp olive oil
½ tsp Maldon salt plus more for sprinkling
4 cups cherry tomatoes, halved
6 mini cucumbers or
   half a long English cucumber, diced
6 radishes, thinly sliced into rounds
⅓ cup basil leaves, torn
⅓ cup mint leaves, torn
⅓ cup cilantro, roughly chopped
½ cup feta, drained and crumbled
¼ cup pistachios, toasted and roughly chopped
½ tsp sumac

method

Za'atar Dressing

Place all dressing ingredients in a jar or a mixing bowl and combine well. Dressing can be refrigerated for up to 2 weeks.

Salad

Preheat oven to 400°F.

Toss pita pieces in olive oil on a large baking sheet and sprinkle with the ½ tsp Maldon salt.

Bake for 2–3 minutes, then flip and bake for another 2–3 minutes until pita pieces are golden and crispy. Set aside.

Combine tomatoes, cucumbers and radishes in a large salad bowl.

Add the herbs and ⅓ of the dressing.

Top with feta, chopped pistachios and pita pieces.

Sprinkle with the sumac and Maldon salt to taste.

Toss well, add more dressing if desired, and serve.

Serve this salad as a complete lunch or pair it with some lamb chops for a perfect dinner!

Heirloom Carrot
Salad

We affectionately call this creation shared by the amazing, lovely Linda "the 12-step salad" because it has so many parts to it! It also has 27 ingredients, but believe me, it's all so worth it. Relax, breathe and complete the 12 steps and you will be enlightened! SERVES 8

ingredients

Roasted Vegetables

10 colourful heirloom carrots, scrubbed and left whole or cut in half lengthwise
1 butternut squash, peeled and cut into 1-inch cubes (skin on is fine)
½ cup olive oil
½ tsp nutmeg
salt and pepper

Salad Topper

½ cup quinoa, cooked and cooled
½ cup rolled oats
¼ cup pine nuts
¼ cup chia seeds
¼ cup vegetable or avocado oil
¼ cup maple syrup
½ tsp salt
½ tsp pepper
½ tsp ground onion
½ tsp paprika

Pickled Red Onion

½ cup apple cider vinegar or white vinegar
¼ cup water
2 tbsp sugar
1 large red onion, halved and thinly sliced

method

Roasted Vegetables

Preheat oven to 400°F.
Toss carrots in half of the olive oil and nutmeg and place on a baking sheet.
Sprinkle with salt and pepper.
Toss squash in remaining olive oil and nutmeg and place on a separate baking sheet.
Sprinkle with salt and pepper.
Put both pans of vegetables in the oven and roast until caramelized, about 35–40 minutes. Set aside.

Dressing

½ cup pancetta, finely diced
1 shallot, finely diced
3 tbsp fresh orange juice
2 tbsp maple syrup
3 tbsp apple cider vinegar
2 tsp Dijon mustard

Salad

6 cups arugula
½ head radicchio, whole leaves or thinly sliced
¼ cup dried cranberries, cherries or pomegranate seeds
½ cup feta or goat cheese, crumbled

Salad Topper

Preheat oven to 325°F.
Combine all salad topper ingredients. Spread onto a parchment lined sheet and roast until golden (20–25 minutes), stirring a few times.
Store in a glass jar in the fridge.

Pickled Red Onion

Combine vinegar, water and sugar in a small pot.
Boil to dissolve sugar. Take off heat and cool slightly.
Pour over sliced red onion.
Let sit for at least 2 hours or make it the day ahead and refrigerate.
Store in a mason jar.

Dressing

Sauté pancetta on medium heat until fat is rendered and pancetta is slightly browned, 3–4 minutes.
Add shallot cook until soft, about 3 minutes.
Add orange juice and reduce slightly.
Add maple syrup, vinegar and Dijon. Keep warm until serving. (Or, make it ahead, refrigerate and reheat.).

to serve

Arrange arugula and radicchio on a platter.
Top with roasted vegetables, cranberries, cheese, some pickled onion, salad topper and dressing.

You can make the salad topper, pickled onion and dressing the day before and then putting the salad together won't be such a project!

Petra's
Preserved Lemon and Crystallized Ginger Salad

Petra is the queen of finding the best recipes and sharing them with me. Then I give them a tweak and my touch. This one is so light and fresh you'll make it over and over again! SERVES 4–6

ingredients

Salad

6–8 cups spicy greens
4 tbsp preserved lemon rinds, finely chopped
4 tbsp crystallized ginger, finely chopped
12 large basil leaves, thinly sliced
4 oz Grana Padano or Parmesan cheese, shaved into thin strips with a mandoline or potato peeler
thick-cut, salted olive oil toast and mashed avocado, to serve (optional)

Shallot Vinaigrette

1 shallot, finely diced
1 tsp Dijon mustard
½ tsp thyme leaves
3 tbsp champagne or white wine vinegar
1 tsp salt
½ tsp pepper
½ cup olive or vegetable oil

method

Shallot Vinaigrette

Combine shallot, Dijon, thyme leaves, vinegar, salt and pepper in a mixing bowl and blend well.
Drizzle in olive oil and whisk until emulsified.
Store in a glass jar with a lid. Shake well before using.

to serve

Combine the greens with the preserved lemon, crystallized ginger, basil and cheese.
Dress right before serving with shallot vinaigrette to taste.

Serve as a side or with avocado toast for a beautiful lunch. You can find the recipe for preserved lemons in this book (page 86) or they can be found in most specialty grocery stores.

Chinese Five-Spice Salad
with Smashed Raspberries and Mangoes

This fun salad pairs beautifully with some barbecued meat or grilled fresh fish.
I make it with mangoes in the winter and peaches in the summertime. SERVES 4

ingredients

2   tbsp apple cider vinegar
1   tsp maple syrup
½   tsp Chinese five-spice powder
1   tbsp olive oil
1   shallot,
     thinly sliced (about ¼ cup)
½   tsp salt
½   cup raspberries
1   mango or 2 peaches,
     thinly sliced
6–8 cups spring greens
     (mizuna and watercress
     are really good)
⅓   cup pistachios, toasted and
     coarsely chopped

method

Mix together vinegar, maple syrup, Chinese five-spice, olive oil, shallot and salt in a large salad bowl.
Add the raspberries to the bowl, lightly crushing them with the back of a fork.
Add the mango and greens and lightly toss.
Top with the toasted pistachios.

Toss in a few blackberries if they're in season for extra flair.
Pairing this salad with the Sweet Steelhead recipe on page 138 is about as good as it gets!

Yuzu
Summer Bowl

Eating these cold noodles on a hot summer's day is so refreshing and satisfying. The yuzu kosho is a Japanese paste made from fermented chilies and yuzu, a citrus fruit that's a more fragrant version of lemon and lime. If you can't find yuzu kosho, a squeeze of lime juice works well too. This bowl is also great with a six-minute egg if prawns aren't your thing. SERVES 4

ingredients

1 pkg (250 g) soba noodles
¼ cup soy sauce
2 tbsp sesame oil
2 tbsp rice wine vinegar
1 tbsp yuzu kosho or lime juice
2 cups spicy greens, spinach or
    watercress, roughly chopped
4 green onions, thinly sliced
2 Persian or mini cucumbers,
    thinly sliced lengthwise or shaved
    with a mandoline or peeler
1 avocado, thinly sliced
¼ cup sesame seeds, toasted
½ cup cilantro leaves and stems,
    chopped
¼ cup mint leaves, torn
12–16 cooked prawns or
    2 cups shrimp meat
1 lime, juice

method

Cook soba noodles according to package instructions.
Drain noodles and rinse under cold water to chill completely.
Pour soy sauce, sesame oil, vinegar and yuzu kosho into a medium bowl and whisk to combine.
Add the soba noodles to the dressing and toss.
Divide the soba noodles among four bowls and top with spicy greens, green onions, cucumbers, avocado, sesame seeds, cilantro, mint and prawns.
Squeeze fresh lime juice over everything.

Bonito flakes are also really yummy sprinkled on this amazing bowl.
They can be found in Nelson at Wings on Baker Street.

Butter Lettuce Salad
with Pickled Radishes and Creamy Feta Dill Dressing

We always have a salad at our house that we refer to as the "house salad." It changes from season to season but usually comes back a few times a year because it's simple and light enough to eat with any dinner. We eat salad after dinner and love to finish with this one.

SERVES 4

ingredients

Dressing

⅓ cup plain yogurt
⅓ cup honey
⅓ cup mayonnaise
⅓ cup sour cream
⅓ cup fresh dill, chopped
⅓ cup feta cheese, crumbled
1   tbsp white wine vinegar or
    fresh lemon juice
1   garlic clove, minced
½ tsp pepper

Salad

6   radishes, thinly sliced
¼ cup rice wine vinegar
1   tsp sugar
1   head butter lettuce,
    torn into large leaves
2   mini cucumbers, thinly sliced
⅓ cup sunflower seeds, toasted
1   avocado, thinly sliced
    or chopped
¼ cup feta, crumbled

method

Dressing

Place the dressing ingredients in a food processor and process until creamy.

Salad

Marinate sliced radishes in vinegar and sugar for 10–15 minutes.
Place lettuce in a shallow salad bowl and top with radishes, cucumbers, sunflower seeds, avocado and feta.
Serve the dressing on the side and drizzle on salad as desired.

*Some salad dressings collapse the lettuce a bit,
so I like to serve them on the side and drizzle just before eating.*

Spiced Lentil
Salade Niçoise

I adore Salade Niçoise and always ordered it for lunch or dinner when I lived in Paris. This version has some wonderfully spiced French Puy lentils and it really completes the protein I always seem to need in every meal. SERVES 4

ingredients

Lentils

1 cup Puy French lentils,
   or any green lentils
salt
½ cup olive oil
2 tsp coriander seeds, crushed
1½ tsp fennel seeds, crushed
1 tsp cumin seeds, crushed
½ tsp red pepper flakes
4 garlic cloves, thinly sliced
1 lemon, about ¼-inch wide strips of zest
   (reserve lemon for salad)
6 small green onions or scallions,
   cut into 2-inch pieces

Salad

4 eggs, cooked for 6 minutes,
   cooled and halved*
8–10 little potatoes, unpeeled,
   cooked, cooled and halved
¼ lb green beans, trimmed, steamed and cooled
1 cup cherry or acorn tomatoes, cut in half
2 anchovy fillets (optional)
1 cup radishes, cut in half
2 cans oil-packed tuna, drained
½ cup fresh herbs, chopped
   (dill, cilantro, tarragon, basil or parsley)
1 lemon
¼ cup extra virgin olive oil
sea salt and freshly ground pepper

method

Lentils

Cook the lentils in a large pot of salted boiling water until just cooked through, 20–30 minutes.
Drain and set aside.
Combine olive oil, coriander, fennel, cumin, red pepper flakes and garlic in a small pot and place over the lowest heat.
Cook oil and spices until oil is fragrant and garlic begins to brown, 10–15 minutes.
Add lemon peel and green onions, cook for another 5 minutes and remove from heat.
Toss lentils with unstrained spiced oil. Transfer to a bowl and cover and chill until needed.

Salad

Place the lentils on each serving plate.
Top with eggs, potatoes, green beans, tomatoes, anchovies, radishes, tuna and chopped herbs.
Squeeze juice of both lemons over salads.
Drizzle with olive oil and season with salt and pepper.

To cook perfect 6-minute eggs, bring a large pot of salted water to a boil. Set eggs in boiling water and cook for 6 minutes. Remove eggs with a slotted spoon and cool in ice water.

Honey Mustard
Brussels Sprouts Slaw

I love Brussels sprouts! The crunchiness of them in this salad with the sweet dried cherries or cranberries gives your jaw a happy workout. I like to eat a big bowl of it for lunch and then carry on with my day. SERVES 4–6

ingredients

Slaw

1   lb Brussels sprouts,
    about 3 cups shaved
⅓   cup slivered almonds, toasted
⅓   cup tart dried cherries
    or cranberries, chopped
⅓   cup Parmesan, grated
2   tbsp flat leaf parsley,
    coarsely chopped

Dressing

2   tbsp apple cider vinegar
1   tbsp Dijon mustard
1   tbsp honey
1   garlic clove, minced
¼   tsp sea salt
¼   cup olive oil

method

Salad

Trim the Brussels sprouts, removing tough outer leaves and ends.

Shave the sprouts lengthwise using a mandoline. This can also be done by hand or in a food processor, but the finished product is not as delicate.

Place all the slaw ingredients in a salad bowl and toss.

Dressing

Place the vinegar, Dijon, honey, garlic and salt in a mixing bowl.

While whisking, gradually drizzle in the olive oil.

Add the dressing to the slaw and toss again.

I like to switch the slaw up. I've added chopped kale, different types of cabbage and herbs like dill and tarragon. Apples or raisins instead of the dried cherries are good too. This salad would also be amazing made with the warm pancetta salad dressing on page 50.

Kale and Cucumber Salad
with Roasted Ginger Dressing

The roasted ginger in this salad dressing is unbelievable! I had never roasted ginger before reading about this technique and now I'm hooked. You will be too. SERVES 4–6

ingredients

Dressing

fresh ginger, skin on (about a 2-inch piece or ½ oz)
1   red Thai chili, seeded and finely chopped,
    or ½ tsp red chili flakes
1   garlic clove
3   tbsp fish sauce
3   tbsp sugar
3   tbsp vegetable oil

Salad

¼   cup shallots, thinly sliced
2   tbsp vegetable oil for frying shallots
1   bunch Red Russian or Tuscan kale, ribs and stems
    removed, torn into bite-size pieces (about 6 cups)
1   long English cucumber, thinly sliced
2   Persian or mini cucumbers, thinly sliced
1   small red onion, thinly sliced
½   lime, juice (about 2 tbsp)
2   tsp sugar
salt and pepper
1   bunch cilantro, chopped

method

Dressing

Preheat broiler and broil ginger, turning once, until dark brown, partly scorched and fully tender (40–50 minutes).
Slice thinly, leaving skin on.
Pulse ginger, other ingredients and 4 tbsp water in a food processor until combined. Set aside.

Salad

Sauté shallots in vegetable oil over medium heat. When crispy and golden, after about 3 minutes, drain them on paper towels.
Massage kale with a ¼ cup of the dressing until slightly softened.
Toss cucumbers, red onion, lime juice and sugar in a medium-size bowl to combine and season with salt and pepper.
Let sit for about 10 minutes to allow the cucumbers to soften slightly.
Add the cucumber and onion marinating mixture to a salad bowl or serving platter with the kale.
Toss to combine, adding more dressing if desired.
Top with cilantro and fried shallots.

We served this salad with the Moroccan-Inspired Short Ribs (page 132) and Gail's Coconut Rice (page 99).
The combination was a total winner!

Edamame Rice Noodle Salad
with Tamarind Dressing

You will be so addicted to this salad! We turn it into a beautiful lunch or dinner, which we call the Kootenay Bowl. You can find it on page 130. SERVES 4–6

ingredients

Salad

250 g pkg rice stick noodles

2 cups edamame beans, cooked and drained

3 green onions, thinly sliced

1 fresh red chili, seeds removed and finely chopped

¼ cup cilantro, coarsely chopped

¼ cup mint leaves, torn

3 tbsp sesame seeds, toasted

Tamarind Dressing

2 tbsp galangal root or ginger, grated

2 garlic cloves, minced

¼ cup fresh lime juice or rice wine vinegar

1 tbsp sesame oil

2 tbsp sugar

2 tsp tamarind concentrate or paste

1 tbsp tamari or soy sauce

1 tsp salt

½ tsp pepper

½ cup vegetable oil

method

Salad

Cook the noodles in a large pot of boiling water for about 5–6 minutes.

Drain and rinse and place on a tea towel until needed.

Cut the cooked noodles with scissors to shorten the strands if desired.

Dressing

Whisk together the dressing ingredients and place in a small bowl or jar.

to serve

Place cooked rice noodles in a large bowl and add edamame beans, green onions, chili, cilantro, mint and toasted sesame seeds.

Drizzle with the dressing and toss to combine.

Place noodles on a serving platter or in a big salad bowl.

Garnish with extra sesame seeds, organic pea shoots, julienned red peppers, whole cilantro leaves and shaved carrots and cucumbers if desired.

Warm Roasted Potato Salad
with Wilted Kale and Creamy Tahini Dressing

The barely wilted kale added to these hot little potatoes is such a treat.
It's a great warm salad served at room temperature, but also excellent as a side dish for any dinner. SERVES 4–6

ingredients

Tahini Dressing

½ cup tahini, well stirred
¼ cup warm water
3 tbsp fresh lemon juice
1 clove garlic, minced
1 tsp sesame oil
1 tsp soy sauce
½ tsp salt

Salad

2 lb (about 6 cups)
   mini potatoes, cut in half
⅓ cup olive oil
salt and pepper
3 cloves garlic, thinly sliced
½ tsp red chili flakes
½ cup Parmesan cheese, grated
1 large bunch kale, stems
   and centre ribs removed,
   thinly sliced

method

Dressing

Purée the dressing ingredients in a blender or food processor.

Add more warm water if the mixture seems too thick.

Salad

Preheat oven to 450°F.

Place rack in upper third of oven.

Toss potatoes with oil and sprinkle with salt and pepper.

Spread evenly on a parchment-lined baking sheet.

Roast for approximately 10–12 minutes, then add garlic and red chili flakes. Stir and roast for another 10 minutes.

Sprinkle with Parmesan and continue roasting until cheese is melted and golden in spots and potatoes are cooked through, about 5 more minutes. Remove from oven.

Add kale to the pan with hot roasted potatoes, mixing well to absorb any of the oil and garlic.

Transfer potatoes and kale to a medium bowl, drizzle with dressing and season with salt and pepper to taste.

We served this salad with Tuscan Split Chicken from Whitewater Cooks at Home
and Conner's Roasted Tomatoes with Anchovy Bread Crumbs found in this book on page 84,
and we all screamed with happiness over this perfect little dinner!

Frisée, Radicchio & Endive Salad
with Blue Cheese & Honey Walnuts

My treasured friend Emmy, who has the best palate of anyone I know, shared this beautiful recipe with me for this collection of salads. She makes it for hundreds of movie crew people and says they go wild for it. The honey walnuts and sweet grapes really give this classic recipe a fun twist. SERVES 4

ingredients

Dressing

- ½ tsp red pepper flakes
- 1 tsp Dijon mustard
- 1 tsp honey
- 1 clove crushed garlic
- 2 tbsp tarragon vinegar or apple cider vinegar
- 6 tbsp extra virgin olive oil

Salad

- ½ cup walnuts, roughly chopped
- 1 tbsp honey
- ½ tsp salt
- 1 head radicchio, leaves separated
- 2 Belgian endives, leaves separated
- 1 small head frisée or escarole lettuce, washed and dried
- ½ bulb fennel, finely sliced on the diagonal
- 2 sprigs of fresh tarragon, leaves
- ¼ cup blue cheese, crumbled
- ½ cup green grapes, halved, or pomegranate seeds

method

Dressing

Place all dressing ingredients except oil in a medium bowl and stir to combine.

Add the olive oil in a slow steady stream, whisking until emulsified.

Salad

Toast the walnuts gently in a pan on medium heat to release the oils and flavour, until just starting to turn golden brown.

Remove from heat and add honey.

Stir until nuts are well coated and place onto a piece of parchment paper.

Salt lightly and allow nuts to cool.

Tear greens into bite-size pieces and place in a large salad bowl.

Mix prepared greens together and toss gently with the dressing.

Top greens with the honey walnuts, tarragon, fennel, blue cheese and grapes or pomegranate seeds.

This is a great salad to pair with a big juicy steak and your favourite baguette!

soups & sides

Spicy Mushroom Soba Noodle Soup
with Tons of Fresh Herbs · 72

Sheri's Fancy Chicken Noodle Soup
with Marinated Fennel and Pernod · 74

Potato, Leek and Artichoke **Chowder** · 76

Roasted Sumac Veggies with Feta and Radishes · 78

Black Bean Coconut Milk Soup · 79

Green **Minestrone** · 80

French Split Pea and Smoked Bacon Soup · 82

Conner's Baked Heirloom Tomatoes
with Anchovy Bread Crumbs · 84

Preserved **Lemons** · 86

Scalloped Potato Gratin
with Truffle Oil and Fresh Sage Leaves · 88

Broccolini with Caramelized Peanuts and Orange Peel · 90

Duncan's **Fancy Greek Potatoes** · 92

Kimchi Fried Rice and Bacon Bowl · 94

Roasted Butternut Squash with Pumpkin Seed Spiced Butter · 96

Bailey's **Cauliflower Rice** · 98

Gail's **Coconut Rice** · 99

Whole Roasted Cauliflower
with Green Sauce and Tahini Drizzle · 100

Spicy Mushroom Soba Noodle Soup
with Tons of Fresh Herbs

The depth and richness of this clear and spicy noodle soup comes from the long sautéing of the mushrooms. Try to find a variety of them for flavour and texture. The vinegar gives it a delicious sourness and the soy sauce gives it a meatiness. If you don't use the optional beef stock, it's also vegan, which I'm not, but you never know what's next! Thanks to Petra for sharing this comforting soup with me. SERVES 4

ingredients

3 tbsp vegetable or olive oil
4 garlic cloves, thinly sliced
2 large shallots, thinly sliced
sea salt and ground black pepper
1½ lbs assorted mushrooms
 (such as oyster, crimini,
 shiitake or porcini), sliced
 or torn into bite size pieces
 (about 6 cups when sliced)
½–¾ tsp red pepper flakes
½ cup soy sauce
¼ cup rice wine vinegar
6 cups water
1 cup beef broth (optional)
8–10 oz soba noodles
 (or any noodle you prefer)
2 cups fresh herbs, leaves and
 stems (mint, cilantro, chives,
 parsley or a mixture),
 for serving
4 tsp toasted sesame seeds,
 for serving
4 tsp sesame oil, for serving
1 red Thai chili pepper, thinly
 sliced for serving if you
 want extra heat!

method

Heat oil in a large pot over medium heat.
Add garlic and shallots and season with salt and pepper.
Stir occasionally until shallots start to turn golden brown, about 3–4 minutes.
Add mushrooms and red pepper flakes and sauté, stirring occasionally, until the mushrooms have softened and turned a deep golden brown, about 10–15 minutes.
Add soy sauce, vinegar, water and beef broth if using.
Reduce heat to a gentle simmer and season with more salt and pepper.
Simmer for about 15–20 minutes to really let the flavours meld.
Taste and if needed, adjust seasonings and add a little more soy sauce and vinegar.
Cook the noodles according to package directions and cool.

to serve

Place noodles in the bottom of each serving bowl.
Ladle the broth and mushrooms into each bowl, evenly divided.
Top with the fresh herbs, sesame seeds and sesame oil.
Garnish with some sliced red Thai chiles if desired.

I've added sautéed tofu to this flavourful bowl of broth, which was so good and gave it some protein.
A raw egg stirred into it is also a great addition!

Sheri's Fancy Chicken Noodle Soup
with Marinated Fennel and Pernod

My talented friend Sheri always shares the best recipes with me for my cookbooks. She has a great palate and is passionate about healthy and delicious food. She loves Italy and France, growing her own vegetables and raising bees. She is my bravest friend who's never afraid to try new adventures. Thanks, Sher. SERVES 4–6

ingredients

Marinated Fennel

2 tbsp extra virgin olive oil
2 tbsp white wine vinegar
¼ tsp salt
½ cup fennel, finely diced, plus a
    handful of minced fennel fronds
1 tbsp fresh tarragon, chopped

Soup

1 tbsp extra virgin olive oil
3 cups fennel bulbs, finely diced
1 leek, finely diced
2 celery stalks, finely diced
2 garlic cloves, minced
½ tsp salt
¼ tsp ground black pepper
2 boneless, skinless chicken breasts,
    chopped into bite-size pieces
½ cup vermouth or Pernod
10 cups low-sodium chicken broth
¼ cup fresh tarragon leaves,
    roughly chopped
2 cups fresh spinach,
    roughly chopped
4 oz angel hair pasta

method

Marinated Fennel

Combine oil, vinegar and salt in a small pot over medium heat.
Bring to a simmer, stirring to dissolve salt.
Place diced fennel, fennel fronds and chopped tarragon in a heatproof jar or container and pour vinegar mixture over top. Let cool at room temperature and refrigerate until needed.

Soup

Heat oil over medium heat. When hot, add fennel, leek, celery, garlic, salt and pepper.
Cook for 10 minutes or until softened and starting to turn golden brown.
Add chicken pieces and cook until chicken has seared a bit, about 5 minutes.
Deglaze pan with the vermouth or Pernod and cook for about 30 seconds.
Add broth and tarragon leaves.
Bring to a boil, then reduce heat to medium.
Simmer, partially covered, for about 20 minutes.
Add spinach and pasta and simmer for 3 minutes or until softened.
Taste and add additional salt and pepper if desired.
Divide soup among the serving bowls and top with the marinated fennel.

Sometimes I float toasted crostini slices and some shaved Parmesan on top of this soup when I want it to be a bit heartier!

Potato, Leek and Artichoke
Chowder

My stepmother, Marcia, shared this awesome soup with me this winter and it's a beauty. It's also vegan for you vegans out there!

SERVES 4–6

ingredients

2 tbsp extra virgin olive oil,
   plus extra for drizzling
3½ cups leeks, white and
   light green parts, diced
½ cup celery, diced
½ cup carrots, diced
½ tsp sea salt
freshly ground black pepper
3 garlic cloves, minced
1½ lbs Yukon Gold potatoes,
   diced (about 2 cups)
4 cups vegetable broth
1 14-oz can artichoke hearts,
   drained and roughly chopped
½ cup raw cashews
1½ tsp Dijon mustard
1 tbsp capers
1 lemon, juice (about 3 tbsp)
½–1 cup water
¼ cup fresh dill, plus more
   for garnish
¼ cup chives or green onions,
   chopped

method

Heat oil in a large pot over medium heat.

Add leeks, celery, carrots, salt and a few grinds of pepper.

Stir occasionally for 8–10 minutes.

Add garlic and sauté 1 minute longer.

Add potatoes and broth and bring to a boil. Reduce heat and simmer 15–20 minutes until potatoes are tender.

Stir in artichokes.

Let cool slightly and transfer ⅓ of the soup to a blender along with cashews, mustard, capers and 1 tbsp lemon juice. Blend until smooth.

Pour back into soup pot and stir in water to thin it out a bit for desired consistency.

Add the dill and remaining 2 tbsp lemon juice.

Season with salt and pepper to taste.

Garnish with dill, chives and a drizzle of olive oil.

This beautiful soup can be served hot or cold.
It's really yummy with some crumbled feta and another squeeze of lemon.

Roasted Sumac Veggies
with Feta and Radishes

The roasted lemon slices, sumac, radishes and feta are what make these roasted veggies different and very yummy.
The healthy and talented Alivia shared this recipe with all of us who are so glad to be together again in the pages of this cookbook!

SERVES 4

ingredients

- 4 lemons, sliced into thin rounds
- 2 tsp turmeric
- 1 tsp sumac
- ½ tsp salt
- 1 tsp black pepper
- 6 tbsp olive oil
- 1 head cauliflower, divided into large florets
- 8 medium carrots, peeled and sliced lengthwise
- 6 whole cloves garlic, skins off and smashed with the back of a knife
- ½ cup feta, crumbled
- 4 medium radishes, thinly sliced

method

Preheat oven to 400°F.

Arrange lemon slices evenly spaced on a large sheet tray.

Place turmeric, sumac, salt, pepper and olive oil in a large bowl and stir to combine. Add cauliflower, carrots and garlic and toss well.

Arrange veggies on top of the lemon slices and bake until edges are crispy and golden brown, about 40 minutes.

Remove from oven and sprinkle feta over top.

Return to oven for 5 minutes, until the feta is slightly melted.

Place veggies on a serving platter and top with radishes.

Garnish with some fresh cilantro or mint if you like!

Black Bean
Coconut Milk Soup

I never get tired of black bean soup! This is a good one, made with coconut milk and chipotle chilies.

SERVES 4-6

ingredients

2   tbsp olive oil
1   medium white onion, finely diced
1   clove garlic, minced
1½ tsp cumin
1½ tsp chipotle chili in adobo sauce,
    finely chopped
2½ cups vegetable stock
2   15-oz cans black beans, rinsed and
    drained (or 3 cups cooked black beans)
1   14-oz can coconut milk
cilantro, diced green onions and
    diced tomatoes, for garnish

method

Heat olive oil in a heavy-bottomed soup pot.
Sauté onion, garlic, cumin and chili for approximately
5 minutes, until golden.
Add ½ cup stock and cook about 2 minutes, until reduced.
Add beans, coconut milk and remaining stock.
Increase heat to high. Once boiling, reduce heat and
simmer for 15 minutes.

Remove from heat and purée with a hand
blender or food processor until smooth.
Return to pot and reheat.
Garnish with cilantro, green onions and
tomatoes.

I like to add a dollop of sour cream and a few crunchy homemade tortilla chips.
You could also make a pot of brown rice and turn this soup into a meal.

Minestrone

Packed full of greens and flavour, you'll love this version of the classic minestrone soup!

SERVES 4-6

ingredients

½ cup packed basil leaves
¼ cup extra virgin olive oil
2 tbsp Italian parsley, chopped
4 cloves garlic, peeled
½ medium onion, cut into chunks
2 medium new red potatoes,
   cut into ½ inch chunks
3 stalks celery, finely diced
2 medium carrots, finely diced
2 large tomatoes, finely diced
4 cups vegetable or chicken stock
2 cups loosely packed spinach,
   trimmed and rinsed
1½ cups canned cannellini beans,
   rinsed
1 cup fresh or frozen baby green peas
½ head frisée lettuce or 2 cups kale,
   cut into bite-size pieces
salt and pepper to taste
¼ cup Parmesan cheese, grated
extra virgin olive oil for drizzling

method

Place ¼ cup basil, 2 tbsp olive oil, parsley, garlic and onions in the bowl of a food processor and process until slightly chunky.

Heat remaining oil over medium-low heat in a large soup pot.

Add herb and garlic mixture and stir until softened and there is no liquid in the pot, about 5 minutes.

Add potatoes, celery, carrots and tomatoes, and cook until vegetables are golden brown, about 6 minutes.

Add the stock and bring to a boil.

Reduce heat to medium low, cover and cook, stirring occasionally until vegetables are tender, about 20 minutes

Stir in spinach, beans, peas and frisée or kale, until greens are just wilted and tender.

Season to taste with salt and pepper and add remaining basil.

Ladle soup into bowls, sprinkle with Parmesan and drizzle with olive oil.

Serve this green beauty with a loaf of our Lovely's Rustic Boulangerie Bread (page 32)
and a hunk of your favourite cheddar.

French Split Pea
and Smoked Bacon Soup

If you don't have a big ham bone, but are in the mood for a thick pea soup with smoky bacon flavour, this is a good one! It's also versatile because you can leave the bacon out to make it vegan. You could serve some crispy bacon bits and a bowl of sour cream on the side and make everyone happy! SERVES 6

ingredients

2   tbsp olive oil
1   cup smoked bacon, diced
1   medium onion, diced
1   large carrot, peeled and diced
2   cloves garlic, minced
1   tbsp fresh thyme leaves,
      chopped
2–3 tsp salt
freshly ground black pepper
1   bay leaf
2   potatoes, peeled and diced
1½ cups dried split peas,
      yellow or green
7–8 cups water or
      vegetable stock
½   cup sherry
pumpkin seeds, bacon bits and
sour cream for garnish if desired

method

Heat the olive oil in a large pot over medium heat.

Add bacon, onion and carrot and cook, stirring frequently, until the onions are soft.

Add the garlic, thyme, salt, a few generous grinds of black pepper, bay leaf, potatoes and split peas.

Add the water or stock and bring to a boil.

Reduce heat to medium-low and cook partially covered to let some of the steam escape, stirring occasionally, until peas and potatoes are very soft, 1½–2 hours.

Add sherry and cook for a few more minutes.

Remove soup from heat, take out the bay leaf and purée in batches to the consistency you desire. I like it a bit chunky.

Add more salt and water if needed.

Garnish with toasted pumpkin seeds, bacon bits and sour cream if desired.

Serve this hearty soup with a loaf of our Rustic Boulangerie Bread (page 32) and some of your favourite triple-cream Brie cheese.

Conner's Baked Heirloom Tomatoes
with Anchovy Bread Crumbs

Yum! Thanks to Conner for inventing this dish when we had some beautiful heirloom tomatoes on the counter and needed something colourful on our plates that night. The best and simplest recipes are often from the ingredients you have on hand. I always have anchovies in my house! SERVES 4

ingredients

3   tbsp olive oil
4   medium heirloom tomatoes,
    quartered, or 8–10 Roma
    tomatoes, halved
1   bunch of basil,
    sliced into thin strips
1   clove garlic, minced
Maldon sea salt
freshly ground black pepper
4   anchovies
1   cup panko bread crumbs

method

Preheat oven to 375°F.

Combine 1 tbsp of the olive oil, tomatoes, half the basil, and minced garlic in a medium-size bowl.

Season with sea salt and pepper to taste.

Place tomato mixture in a small baking dish and bake for 25–30 minutes.

Heat remaining 2 tbsp olive oil in a skillet over medium-high heat.

Add anchovies and lightly mash them with a wooden spoon in the hot oil until they form a paste.

Add bread crumbs to the pan and toss to coat in oil.

Cook, stirring occasionally, for 5–7 minutes or until bread crumbs are golden brown. Remove from heat.

Season bread crumbs with more salt and pepper and set aside.

Remove tomatoes from oven and top with bread crumbs and remaining basil.

These tomatoes are really good served
with a split barbecued chicken and a salad of spicy greens.

Preserved
Lemons

Having a jar of preserved lemons in the fridge makes me feel so smitten with myself! Preserved lemons are one of the most indispensable ingredients of Moroccan cooking. A little dice or rounds of these beauties can add the best flavour to everything from lamb dishes, vegetables, rice, sauces and salads, to panna cotta and muffins!

MAKES 1 LARGE MASON JAR

ingredients

6 lemons
6 tbsp coarse sea salt
2 rosemary sprigs
1 large red chili pepper
6 lemons, juice
olive oil for topping up

method

Sterilize a jar large enough to fit the lemons. To sterilize, fill it with boiling water, leave for a minute, then empty it and let it dry without wiping.

Wash the lemons and slice the tip off of each.

Cut a deep cross all the way from the top of each lemon to within 2 cm of the base.

Stuff each lemon with 1 tbsp of salt and place in jar.

Push the lemons in tightly so they're squeezed together.

Seal the jar and leave at room temperature for a week.

Remove the lid after this initial period and press the lemons as hard as you can to squeeze the liquid out, leaving the lemons and their juice in the jar.

Add the rosemary, chili pepper and lemon juice. Cover with a thin layer of olive oil and place in the fridge.

Refrigerate for four weeks before using.

The trick is to keep making a new jar as you are using the previous one,
so you never run out!

Scalloped Potato Gratin
with Truffle Oil and Fresh Sage Leaves

This is the most delicious version of scalloped potatoes I have ever eaten! It's more like a potato tart or potatoes dauphinoise than the traditional scalloped potatoes. It's really good to eat the next day with a salad for lunch. My kids made these at Easter this year and we were hooked! SERVES 8–10

ingredients

¼ cup unsalted butter, room temperature, plus more for greasing the tinfoil

3 cups whipping cream

¼ cup fresh sage leaves, chopped

4 large garlic cloves, finely grated or minced

¼ tsp nutmeg

1½ tsp salt

5 large eggs

4 lbs russet potatoes (about 6 large or 8 medium), peeled and set in a bowl of cold water

freshly ground black pepper

2¼ cups Gruyère cheese, grated

1 tsp truffle oil (if desired)

sage leaves, finely chopped, for garnish

method

Preheat oven to 350°F.

Brush ¼ cup butter on a 9 x 13-inch baking sheet and also brush one or two pieces of tin foil with more butter. Set the foil aside.

Bring the cream, sage, garlic, nutmeg and a pinch of salt to a simmer on medium heat, then simmer until reduced by a quarter, about 15 minutes.

Beat eggs lightly in a large heatproof bowl. Beating constantly, gradually add a little of the hot cream, then slowly pour in the rest of the cream, whisking to prevent eggs from curdling. Set aside.

Slice the potatoes with a mandoline or very sharp knife into ⅛-inch thick rounds.

Arrange one layer of potatoes on the buttered baking sheet, slightly overlapping the slices. Sprinkle with ¾ tsp of the salt and some freshly ground black pepper.

Pour half of the egg mixture over the potatoes, then top with ½ cup of the cheese.

Repeat the layers of potato, seasoning and egg mixture.

Top with the remaining 1¾ cups cheese.

Cover the baking sheet with the foil, buttered side down, and bake for 20 minutes.

Remove the foil and bake until the potatoes and cheese are browned and bubbling, 25–30 minutes.

Let cool slightly. Drizzle lightly with truffle oil, scatter with fresh sage and cut into squares and serve.

You can assemble the gratin up to 4 hours before baking it. Just store it loosely covered in the fridge. The gratin can also be baked 4 hours ahead, kept uncovered at room temperature and then reheated in a 450°F oven until the top is shiny.

Broccolini
with Caramelized Peanuts and Orange Peel

These yummy caramelized peanuts are a really fresh addition to any steamed green vegetables.
The inspiration for this comes from the king of all vegetables, Yotam Ottolenghi.

SERVES 4

ingredients

3 tbsp peanut oil
1 tbsp fresh ginger,
    peeled and grated
3 garlic cloves, thinly sliced
¼ cup shallot, thinly sliced
1 orange, julienned peel
4 tbsp unsalted peanuts
1½ tsp honey
2 tbsp soy sauce
1 lb broccolini

method

Heat the oil in a small saucepan over medium-high heat.

Add the ginger, garlic, shallot, orange peel and peanuts and fry for 2–3 minutes, stirring frequently, until the ginger, garlic and nuts are light golden brown.

Turn off the heat and add the honey and soy sauce.

Steam broccolini for 4–5 minutes until tender.

Remove from heat and place in a serving dish.

Drizzle with the sauce, toss and serve.

*This is really good made with gai lan, bok choy, green beans
or any of your favourite green vegetables!*

Duncan's
Fancy Greek Potatoes

Duncan is Conner's friend from his days at McGill University and they share a mutual love of cooking. These are Duncan's "fancy potatoes." They're delicious and can be served with just about anything! The Buttermilk Chicken (page 122) or the Pan-Roasted Lamb recipe (page 116) are two of our favourites to pair them with. SERVES 4

ingredients

6–7 red or white waxy potatoes,
   peeled, cut into medallions
   about 2 inches thick
   (ends removed)
salt and pepper
1 tbsp olive oil
2 tbsp butter
3–4 garlic cloves, crushed
6 thyme sprigs or rosemary
   or oregano branches
   (or a combination)
¾ cup white wine
¾ cup chicken stock
1 lemon, juice, plus more
   for serving

method

Preheat oven to 400°F.

Soak potato medallions in a large bowl of cold water to remove starch, about 15 minutes.

Remove medallions from water, place on a paper towel or clean tea towel and pat dry.

Sprinkle some salt and pepper on one side of the potatoes.

Place the oil and butter in a 9–10-inch cast-iron pan and turn heat to medium.

Fry medallions salted side down for about 5 minutes until lightly browned.

Season top side of potatoes with salt and pepper. Flip and fry for another 5 minutes until lightly browned.

Add the garlic to the pan.

Add the thyme sprigs and push the potatoes down into the fat.

Add the wine and reduce for a few seconds.

Add the chicken stock and lemon juice. The liquid should come ⅔ of the way up the medallions.

Put in the oven and cook for 45 minutes.

Remove from oven and squeeze fresh lemon juice on them before serving.

The crust on these potatoes and the liquid that has soaked into the flesh
make these potatoes so divine. Thanks, Duncan!

Kimchi Fried Rice
and Bacon Bowl

I hadn't eaten much kimchi until recently, but now really love this fried rice with kimchi and lots of bacon! It's a great thing to do with any leftover rice, farro, quinoa or whatever grains you choose, and makes for an awesome lunch. SERVES 4

ingredients

8 slices thick-cut bacon, diced
2 cloves garlic, minced
1 medium white onion, diced
2 tbsp ginger, peeled and grated
1 tbsp gochujang
2 cups kimchi, drained slightly
4 cups cooked basmati or
  jasmine rice (day-old is fine),
  or any grains of choice
2 tbsp toasted sesame oil
1 tbsp fish sauce
2 green onions, chopped
2 tbsp sesame seeds, toasted
4 eggs
2 sheets nori, julienned
  with scissors

method

Place bacon in a cold wok or large skillet, turn heat to medium and cook until the fat has rendered.

Add garlic, onion and ginger and cook until bacon is crisp and onions are translucent.

Add gochujang and kimchi to the pan and stir until gochujang has evenly dispersed throughout the dish.

Add rice and sesame oil, mixing to incorporate, stirring occasionally and allowing flavours to meld together, 1–2 minutes.

Stir in fish sauce and turn heat off or to very low.

Fry eggs while kimchi rice is cooking.

Dish rice into four bowls and top with green onions, sesame seeds, fried eggs, and julienned nori.

I like to make this in the morning and then all that's left is to fry the eggs.
Try adding 2 cups of fresh spinach leaves to the kimchi rice after you
turn the heat off so it just wilts. It goes so well with the bacon in this dish!
Gochujang can be found in Nelson at Wings Grocery on Baker Street.

Roasted Butternut Squash
with Pumpkin Seed Spiced Butter

Eating this squash reminds me of eating dessert with dinner! Serve it with something plain like roasted chicken or lamb chops and you'll see what I mean. You could use any kind of squash and switch up the seeds, but the main thing is the browned butter with the spices and the bed of yogurt it's nestled into. The combination of the flavourful butter and yogurt is to die for! SERVES 4–6

ingredients

1   butternut squash
    (skin on is fine),
    cut into 1-inch chunks
3   tbsp olive oil
Maldon salt and freshly ground
    black pepper
½ cup unsalted butter
¼ cup pumpkin seeds, toasted
½ tsp cumin
½ tsp turmeric
¼ tsp cinnamon
¼ tsp red pepper flakes
½ tsp Maldon salt
1   cup full-fat Greek yogurt
2   tbsp fresh lemon juice

method

Preheat oven to 425°F.

Toss squash with olive oil and salt and pepper and place on a parchment-lined baking sheet.

Roast until squash is totally tender and slightly caramelized, about 40–50 minutes.

Melt the butter in a small pot over medium heat and cook, swirling the pan occasionally, until butter has browned and started to foam (about 3–5 minutes).

Remove from heat and add pumpkin seeds, cumin, turmeric, cinnamon, red pepper flakes and ½ tsp salt. Set aside.

Combine yogurt and lemon juice in a small bowl and season with a bit of salt.

Spoon the yogurt sauce onto the bottom of a large serving platter or bowl.

Arrange squash chunks nestled into each other and drizzle with the pumpkin seed butter.

Top with a bit more flaky salt and freshly ground black pepper.

You can roast the squash several hours ahead of time and keep it loosely wrapped at room temperature. It doesn't need to be reheated because the warm butter will heat it up.

Bailey's
Cauliflower Rice

Conner's friend Bailey really knows and loves good food.
The flavourings in her Cauliflower Rice are perfectly balanced and really complement the delicious cauliflower. SERVES 4

ingredients

2 tbsp olive oil
3 cloves garlic, minced
1 tbsp ginger, peeled and grated
¼ cup sweet onion, diced
½ tsp cinnamon
½ tsp chili powder
1 tsp cumin
¼ tsp allspice
¼ tsp red chili flakes
1 whole cauliflower, finely grated
    to the size of rice or pulsed
    in small batches in a food
    processor (about 4–5 cups)
½ lemon, juice
salt and pepper to taste
cilantro, for garnish

method

Heat olive oil in a skillet over medium heat.

Add garlic, ginger and onion and cook until onion is translucent.

Add spices and cook until fragrant, about a minute.

Add cauliflower and cook for two minutes, stirring often.

Reduce the heat to medium-low and cover with a lid (preferably one that's too small for the skillet, so it sits directly on top of cauliflower rice).

Cook covered for 8–10 minutes, until the bottom of the cauliflower rice is golden and crispy.

Remove the lid, add lemon juice and season with salt and pepper.

Garnish with some cilantro leaves or whole sprigs if desired.

Turn over with a spatula or stir with a wooden spoon and serve.

I love this cauliflower rice served with just about anything!
Bailey and Raafy love it with meatballs.

soups & sides

Gail's
Coconut Rice

Gaily makes the best food! Her back country ski lodge and Haida Gwaii boating trip guests are so lucky to have her. Here is her perfect coconut rice recipe. It pairs well with many Thai, Korean and Chinese dinners, or any meal you need to perk up with some flavourful rice. SERVES 4

ingredients

1 cup coconut milk
1 cup water
½ tsp salt
1 cup basmati rice
1 tbsp toasted coconut ribbons, for garnish
1 tsp fresh ginger, grated, for garnish
1 tsp green onions, chopped, for garnish
1 tsp cilantro, chopped, for garnish

method

Bring coconut milk and water to a boil and add salt.
Stir in the basmati rice and bring back to a boil.
Turn the heat down to a simmer and cover.
Cook for 15 minutes, then remove from heat and let steam for 10 minutes.
Garnish with coconut ribbons, ginger, green onions and cilantro if desired.

You can freeze the extra coconut milk for another use.
You can also easily make this in a rice cooker. I'm a big fan of using a rice cooker!

Whole Roasted Cauliflower
with Green Sauce and Tahini Drizzle

This is a thing of beauty to me. When I was young, my Mom used to roast a whole head of cauliflower with hot garlic butter for dipping as an after-school treat. I'd be so embarrassed when my friends saw what strange snacks she made. She was ahead of her time! To take this beautiful whole roasted cauliflower to the next level, top it with pomegranate seeds and toasted pine nuts! SERVES 4

ingredients

Cauliflower
1 large cauliflower (with leaves left on)
3 tbsp unsalted butter, room temperature
2 tbsp olive oil
1½ tsp Maldon or flaky sea salt
1 lemon, cut into wedges to serve
¼ cup pomegranate seeds, for garnish (optional)
¼ cup pinenuts, toasted, for garnish (optional)

Green Sauce — Makes 2 cups
1 2-oz tin flat anchovy fillets, drained
½ cup chopped parsley
2 tbsp red wine vinegar
1 lemon, zest
2 tbsp chopped fresh chives or shallots
1 tbsp drained and rinsed capers
¾ cup mayonnaise
¾ cup plain yogurt
freshly ground pepper

Tahini Drizzle
½ cup tahini, well stirred
¼ cup warm water
3 tbsp fresh lemon juice
1 tsp sesame oil
1 tsp soy sauce
½ tsp salt

method

Cauliflower
Preheat oven to 375°F.
Trim the cauliflower leaves with kitchen scissors, leaving about 2 inches.
Fill a pan big enough to fit the cauliflower ¾ full with salted water.
Bring to a boil, then carefully lower in the cauliflower top-down, leaving a bit of the base showing.
Return to a boil and cook for 6 minutes. Use a slotted spoon to transfer cauliflower top-down into a colander. Set aside for 10 minutes to drain.
Mix together butter and olive oil.
Place cauliflower on a medium sized parchment-lined baking sheet, top up, and spread butter-olive oil mixture all over the cauliflower. Sprinkle with sea salt.
Place in the oven and roast for 1½–2 hours, basting the cauliflower with the pan drippings 5 or 6 times, until tender and dark golden brown.
Remove from the oven, set aside for 5 minutes, and then cut it into wedges.

Green Sauce
Place anchovies, parsley, vinegar, lemon zest, chives or shallots, and capers into a blender or food processor and purée until the mixture has nearly liquified (about 3 minutes).
Add the mayonnaise and yogurt and pulse to combine.
Season with freshly ground pepper to taste.

Tahini Drizzle
Place all tahini drizzle ingredients in a food processor and process until smooth and well combined.

to serve

Arrange the cauliflower on a pretty platter with the Green Sauce and Tahini Drizzle in little dishes and lemon wedges on the side.

This beautiful cauliflower can be cut into quarters and served as a side with any grilled meat or fish.
The Green Sauce is also very versatile and can be a dip for any kind of vegetable or chips.

dinners

Chicken with Harissa-Charred Acorn Tomatoes
and Creamy Coconut Celery Root Purée

My son, Conner, and his treasured friends Raafy and Bailey love cooking together and sharing recipes. They don't live in the same city but they pick a recipe once a week, make it on the same night and Facetime their finished dishes and critiques. Here's one they made that we all loved! SERVES 6

ingredients

Celery Root Purée

2   tbsp unsalted butter
5   cups celery root, cut into
    ½-inch cubes (about 1 large
    or 2 medium celery roots)
1½ cups chicken stock
1½ cups coconut milk
1   tsp salt
1   tsp freshly ground pepper

Harissa Chicken

6   chicken thighs, bone in,
    skin on
2   tsp Maldon salt
1   tsp crushed fennel seeds
3   tbsp olive oil
2½ cups cherry or
    acorn tomatoes
3   tbsp harissa paste
3   tbsp red wine vinegar
½   cup feta cheese, crumbled
4   sprigs oregano, leaves,
    plus some sprigs for garnish

Sometimes it's not that easy to find celery root, so we've tried the purée with cauliflower, parsnips, turnips and potatoes, all with delicious results!

method

Celery Root Purée

Melt butter in a heavy-bottomed saucepan over medium-high heat.

Add cubed celery root, stir to coat with butter and cook for 4–5 minutes, stirring often.

Reduce heat to medium-low and cook until lightly browned, about 8–10 minutes, stirring occasionally.

Add chicken stock, coconut milk, salt and pepper to the saucepan.

Bring to a simmer, reduce heat and cook uncovered for 15–20 minutes or until celery root pieces are very tender and liquids are slightly reduced.

Remove from heat and place in a food processor. Process until smooth, about 30 seconds.

Return to the saucepan and keep warm over very low heat until ready to serve, or let it cool and reheat it in the microwave or oven before serving.

Harissa Chicken

Preheat oven to 400°F.

Pat chicken thighs dry with a paper towel. Season on both sides with salt.

Sprinkle with crushed fennel seeds.

Heat oil in a large skillet over medium-high heat.

Sear thighs skin-side-down, completely undisturbed, until skin is golden and crispy, about 10–12 minutes.

Turn chicken over and cook for an additional 5 minutes.

Remove chicken and let rest on a plate or wire baking rack.

Add the tomatoes, harissa paste and vinegar to the same skillet, using leftover oil from chicken.

Cook until tomatoes start to char and burst, about 8–10 minutes.

Return the chicken thighs skin-side-up to the pan, nestling among the tomatoes.

Finish chicken in oven for 15–20 minutes, or until juices run clear.

Remove chicken from the oven, then sprinkle feta and oregano leaves on tomatoes and return to oven for 5 minutes.

To serve, top celery root purée with chicken thighs, harissa tomatoes and plenty of sauce from the skillet.

Garnish with oregano sprigs.

Black Bean Grilled Flank Steak
with Nuoc Cham Sauce

Flank steak is my best friend in the summer. It loves a good marination overnight, is flavourful and inexpensive, and feeds six people! What's not to love! This version, paired with a light and spicy Nuoc Cham Sauce, is perfect on a hot summer night … or a chilly winter evening! SERVES 4–6

ingredients

1 flank steak, about 1 kg (2 lbs)

Black Bean Marinade

½ cup fermented black beans, rinsed
4 cloves garlic, minced
1 tbsp ginger, peeled and grated
1 cup cilantro, chopped
⅓ cup canola oil
½ cup soy sauce
¼ cup ketchup
¼ cup hoisin sauce
¼ cup rice wine vinegar

Nuoc Cham Sauce

1–2 Thai red chili peppers, seeded (or more, depending on how hot you like your food!)
1 tbsp ginger, peeled and grated
2 cloves garlic, peeled and minced
1½ tbsp sugar
½ cup cilantro stems, chopped
¼ cup fish sauce
1 tbsp rice wine vinegar
½ cup water
2 limes, zest and juice
1 cup cilantro leaves, chopped

method

Black Bean Marinade

Place rinsed fermented black beans in a bowl.

Pour 1½ cups hot water over beans and let sit for 15 minutes.

Drain beans in a colander and place them in a blender.

Add the garlic, ginger, cilantro, oil, soy sauce, ketchup, hoisin sauce and rice wine vinegar.

Blend until smooth.

Place the flank steak in a baking dish and pour the marinade over top.

Cover with plastic wrap and refrigerate for 4–6 hours or overnight at the most.

Nuoc Cham Sauce

Put the chili, ginger, garlic, sugar and chopped cilantro stems in a bowl and process with a hand blender (or use a mortar and pestle) until well combined.

Add the fish sauce, vinegar, water, lime zest and juice, and chopped cilantro leaves. Stir.

Store the sauce in the fridge in a container with a lid. Shake before serving.

Preheat barbecue to high heat. (You can also use a cast-iron grill pan on the stovetop.)

Lightly oil the grill.

Remove flank steak from marinade. Turn barbecue down to medium and grill the steak for about 7–8 minutes per side, brushing with more marinade while cooking.

Remove from heat and let it rest, loosely covered in tinfoil, for at least ten minutes and up to half an hour before slicing.

Slice flank steak diagonally across the grain as thinly as you can.

Place steak on a serving platter and pour any juices from the carving board over the steak.

Drizzle with some of the Nuoc Cham Sauce and serve with a little bowl on the side.

Gail's Coconut Rice (page 99) or the Edamame Rice Noodle Salad (page 64) would be perfect with this delicious flank steak.

Roasted Salmon
with Curry Sumac Butter

This buttery salmon with slow-roasted vegetables makes for a beautiful one-pan, healthy midweek dinner.

SERVES 4

ingredients

- 1 fennel bulb, thinly sliced
- 1 red onion, cut into 12 wedges
- 1 head cauliflower, cut into florets
- 3 tbsp extra virgin olive oil
- 1½ tsp Maldon or kosher salt
- 4 tbsp unsalted butter
- 2 garlic cloves, crushed
- 1 tbsp ginger, peeled and finely grated or microplaned
- 1 tsp curry powder
- ½ tsp sumac powder
- 4 6-oz portions of salmon, skin on or off
- fresh mint, roughly chopped, for serving

method

Preheat oven to 425°F.

Combine fennel, red onion, cauliflower and oil on a baking pan lined with parchment paper and toss a bit.

Season with salt and roast for 30–35 minutes until vegetables are browned and softened, turning them twice.

Remove from the oven, set aside and reduce temperature to 350°F.

Melt the butter in a small saucepan over medium heat and add garlic, ginger, curry, sumac and a pinch of salt.

Simmer until lightly browned, about one minute, and remove from heat.

Season salmon with salt and lay on top of cooked vegetables (skin-side-down if skin is on).

Drizzle salmon with curry butter.

Return fish and vegetables to the oven and roast for 12–15 minutes or until salmon is just cooked.

Garnish with fresh mint.

I like to serve this dish with Gail's Coconut Rice (page 99). Yum!

Cast-Iron Chicken

Marie made this at a dinner on Hornby Island one summer and we all loved it! It has few ingredients and uses just one pan, so it was perfect for her rental cabin without much kitchen equipment. It was also perfect for Ali and Joel, law school students without a lot of spare time or money, who needed a one-pan dinner! SERVES 4

ingredients

- 2 tbsp olive oil
- 5–6 chicken thighs, bone in and skin on
- 2 tsp herbes de Provence
- 1 tbsp Maldon sea salt
- 10–12 little potatoes, whole or halved
- 12 olives (any large green ones)
- ½ lemon, cut into wedges
- 6 cloves garlic, skins off, whole
- 1 cup canned artichokes, halved (optional)
- ½ cup chicken stock
- ½ cup white wine
- 2 thyme branches
- 2 rosemary sprigs
- ¼ cup parsley, chopped

method

Preheat oven to 400°F

Heat a large cast-iron pan over medium-high heat and add olive oil.

Sprinkle herbes de Provence and sea salt on chicken thighs.

Cook chicken skin-side-down for 5 minutes until browned, then flip and cook for another 5 minutes.

Remove chicken and set aside.

Add the potatoes, olives, lemon, garlic and artichokes to the pan and cook until browned.

Add chicken stock and white wine and bring to a boil.

Return chicken to the pan and add the thyme and rosemary.

Place in the preheated oven and cook for approximately 30 minutes or until potatoes are tender and chicken is done.

Garnish with fresh parsley.

Any of the salads in this book would be perfect with Marie's chicken.

Crispy-Skinned
Fish

I always wanted to know how to get the skin of the fish so crispy and, at the same time, have perfectly cooked fish.
This technique, along with the scrumptious green sauce, is my new go-to for any fish with skin. SERVES 4

ingredients

- 2 anchovy fillets (oil-packed)
- 1 small garlic clove, minced
- 1 cup tender herbs
   (such as parsley, dill or basil),
   roughly chopped
- 1 tbsp capers, chopped
- 2 tbsp fresh lemon juice
   or white wine vinegar
- ½ tsp pepper
- 6 tbsp extra virgin olive oil
- 4 6–oz fish fillets, skin on
   (Arctic char, steelhead,
   ling cod or salmon)
- 1 tbsp Maldon sea salt

method

Mash anchovies and minced garlic on a cutting board until a coarse paste forms.
Transfer to a medium-size bowl and add herbs, capers, lemon juice, pepper and 5 tbsp oil. Combine well.
Swirl remaining 1 tbsp oil in a large non-stick skillet to coat.
Season fish with a bit of salt on both sides and lay skin-side-down in a cold skillet.
Place the skillet over medium heat and let it gradually heat up until fat starts to cook out of the fish, about 4 minutes.
Press gently on fish so the skin is flat against the pan.
Continue to cook until skin is super-crisp and flesh is mostly opaque, 8–12 minutes longer, depending on the thickness of the fish. Increase or decrease heat slightly if needed, but don't try to rush it. You can also add a little more oil to the pan if the skin isn't getting crisp enough.
Turn fish and cook until just opaque all the way through, about 1 minute.

to serve

Spoon green sauce onto a platter or 4 plates and set fish skin-side-up on top.

*I love to eat this fish and sauce with some simply steamed new potatoes,
with butter of course!*

Turkey Burgers

Thanks to Sheri for sharing these delicious gems inspired by Dianne Clement's recipe. She takes them ski touring and I can't quite figure out how she cooks them up there in a remote hut, but Sheri is one talented girl so it doesn't surprise me! These burgers are super-easy with flavourings that evoke memories of Morocco. We all need a good burger once in a while! MAKES 4 PATTIES

ingredients

- ½ cup onion, roughly chopped
- ½ cup dried apricots, roughly chopped
- 2 tbsp pistachios or pine nuts
- 2 cloves garlic
- 1 tsp cayenne pepper
- ½ tsp cumin
- ½ tsp coriander
- ¼ tsp cinnamon
- ½ tsp salt
- ½ tsp pepper
- 1½ pounds ground turkey
- 2 tbsp olive oil
- 4 of your favourite hamburger buns

method

Put the onion, apricots, pistachios, garlic and all the spices in a food processor and pulse until well blended.

Transfer to a large bowl and add the ground turkey.

Combine until well blended.

Form into 4 patties (don't make them too thin).

Brush with olive oil and barbecue or fry them for 6 minutes per side.

Toast the buns.

We like to eat these burgers with caramelized onions, chutney, curried mayonnaise, lettuce and tomatoes. Brioche buns are the best!

Pan-Roasted Herb-Crusted Lamb
with Eggplant, Tomatoes, Olives and Mint Oil

We fiddled with a few different rack of lamb recipes to come up with this version. It has a Moroccan and Mediterranean feel to it. It can be made early and roasted later — always a good thing when you're having guests and want to chill a bit or get the other courses and cocktails ready before they arrive! SERVES 4

ingredients

2 racks of lamb, French trimmed, cut in half or left whole
4 tbsp Dijon mustard

Spice Rub

1 tbsp paprika
1 tbsp sea salt
1 tsp cumin
1 tsp coriander
1 tsp black pepper
½ tsp cinnamon
¼ tsp cayenne pepper

Herb and Panko Crumb Crust Mixture

⅔ cup cilantro, chopped
⅔ cup parsley, chopped
1–2 lemons, juice (about ½ cup)
2 tbsp olive oil
3 medium garlic cloves, minced
½ cup panko crumbs
pinch of salt

Eggplant and Tomatoes

2 Japanese or 1 large eggplant, sliced 1-inch thick
¼ cup extra virgin olive oil
sea salt and freshly ground black pepper
4–6 ripe Roma tomatoes, cut in half lengthwise
6 cloves garlic, roughly chopped
8 large basil leaves, torn
½ cup pitted kalamata olives

Mint Oil

1 cup fresh mint, chopped
1 tsp salt
1 tsp sugar
2 tbsp red wine vinegar
½ cup extra virgin olive oil

method

Spice Rub

Combine all spice rub ingredients in a small bowl.

Rub mixture all over lamb and set aside.

Herb and Panko Crumb Crust Mixture

Combine all herb crust ingredients in a small bowl and set aside.

Lamb

Preheat grill pan for 5 minutes on medium-high heat.

Add 2 tbsp oil to the hot pan.

Sear spice-rubbed lamb racks until brown on both sides. Set aside.

Coat the top side of lamb racks with the Dijon mustard, about 2 tbsp per piece.

Press herb and panko crumb mixture carefully into the mustard on each rack and set aside.

Eggplant, Tomatoes and Lamb

Preheat oven to 425°F.

Brush the eggplant slices all over with olive oil, and season with salt and pepper.

Fry on both sides in a grill pan or non-stick pan over medium heat until lightly coloured.

Remove eggplant from the pan and place around the outside of a roasting pan.

Arrange halved tomatoes beside eggplant.

Sprinkle the vegetables with the garlic, torn basil leaves, salt and pepper.

Drizzle with a little more olive oil, and top with the olives.

Place the lamb crust-side-up in the centre of the pan.

Roast in the preheated oven for about 30 minutes for medium rare.

Remove from the oven, cover and allow lamb to rest for 10 minutes.

Mint Oil

Combine the mint, salt, sugar and vinegar in a blender and blend until smooth.

Add the extra virgin olive oil and mix until well combined.

Slice the lamb into chops, surround it with the vegetables and drizzle it with the mint oil. This lovely dinner would be great served with couscous or Duncan's Fancy Greek Potatoes (page 92).

Claire's Couscous-Stuffed Roasted Chicken
with Green Olive Salsa

Clairence, as I like to affectionately call her, is the best cook and baker and lover of making life so beautiful and fun! She and her husband, Ross, really know how to live each day like they're on a dreamy holiday, which is a pretty amazing thing. The green olive salsa is to die for as a dressing on your favourite greens. SERVES 4-6

ingredients

Couscous Stuffing

1 tsp olive oil
1 medium onion, chopped
1½ cups chicken stock
¼ cup olive oil, plus extra for drizzling
1 lemon, zest and juice
1 cup couscous
½ cup slivered almonds, toasted
1 cup dates, finely chopped
½ cup dried apricots, finely chopped
1 tsp cinnamon
1 tsp smoked paprika
1 egg, lightly beaten

Green Olive Salsa

1½ cups pitted green olives,
    coarsely chopped (Castelvetrano
    or Cerignola if possible)
⅓ cup olive oil
1 tbsp apple cider vinegar
1 shallot, finely chopped
1 red chili pepper, seeded and finely
    chopped, or ¼ tsp red chili flakes
¼ cup Italian parsley, coarsely chopped
¼ cup fresh mint, coarsely chopped

Chicken

1 chicken (about 3½ pounds)
2 tbsp butter, room temperature
20 baby vine tomatoes
1 tbsp olive oil

method

Couscous Stuffing

Heat oil in a small frying pan.

Cook onion, stirring until soft. Remove from heat.

Combine stock, olive oil, lemon zest and juice in a medium saucepan and bring to a boil. Remove from heat.

Add couscous to the stock mixture. Cover and let stand for about 5 minutes until liquid is absorbed, fluffing occasionally with a fork.

Stir in sautéed onion, nuts, dates, apricots, spices and egg and mix well.

Green Olive Salsa

Combine all ingredients and set aside.

Chicken

Preheat oven to 400°F.

Pat chicken dry with paper towels.

Fill the cavity with couscous stuffing.

Set the chicken in a roasting pan, rub all over with butter and sprinkle with salt and pepper.

Roast for 15 minutes.

Reduce oven temperature to 350°F.

Roast for 90 minutes or until cooked through.

Remove chicken from the oven and let rest for 20 minutes.

Place tomatoes on a baking sheet, drizzle with olive oil and roast for about 20 minutes while chicken is resting.

Serve the chicken with the roasted tomatoes, green olive salsa and couscous.

You can also put any extra couscous in a heatproof dish, cover and heat it in the oven for 30 minutes while the chicken and then tomatoes are roasting.

Blake's Pan-Seared Halibut
with Tomatoes, Basil and Feta

My friend Blake used to be a real fisherman for years and years. This is one of his many preparations of his favourite species. You could also make it with cod or red snapper, but fresh halibut is the best treat. SERVES 4

ingredients

3 tbsp olive oil
4 6-oz fillets of halibut, skin on
salt and pepper for seasoning
4 cloves garlic, minced
4–6 vine tomatoes, diced
½ cup white wine (optional)
½ cup fresh basil, thin chiffonade
½ cup feta cheese, crumbled
1 lemon, for squeezing

method

Heat oil in a heavy-bottomed frying pan over medium-high heat
until oil is hot, but not smoking.
Season fish with salt and pepper.
Place the fish skin-side-up and fry until partially cooked and golden in colour,
about 4 minutes.
Flip fish and place garlic, tomatoes, wine, basil and feta around the fish.
Cover with a lid and cook until fish is cooked through,
about 10–12 minutes, depending on the thickness of your fillet.
The tomatoes should be hot and the feta partially melted.

Squeeze lemon juice over the fish.
Serve with basmati rice
and pour all the pan juices
from the fish over the rice.

The halibut will continue to cook a bit after you remove it from the heat,
so be sure to take it off the heat just when it's starting to look opaque and flaky.

dinners

Buttermilk Chicken
with Rosemary and Honey

My dear friend Susie made this for a beautiful and festive dinner at her house last fall and I loved it. The chicken is so moist because the buttermilk tenderizes it as it marinates. Susie's starter was the Rustic Tomato Tarts from *Whitewater Cooks at Home* and dessert was Joey's Apple Cake from the first book, *Whitewater Cooks Pure, Simple and Real Creations*. Thanks, Susie! SERVES 4

ingredients

8–10 chicken thighs,
    bone in, skin on
2 cups buttermilk
¼ cup plus 2 tbsp vegetable oil,
    divided
2 cloves garlic, lightly crushed
1 tbsp black pepper,
    freshly ground
1 tbsp Maldon or any other
    sea salt
2 tbsp fresh rosemary, chopped
1 tbsp honey

method

Place chicken thighs in a ceramic bowl.

Add buttermilk, ¼ cup oil, garlic, pepper, salt, rosemary and honey.

Cover and refrigerate overnight or up to 2 days.

Preheat oven to 400°F.

Remove chicken from marinade and place on a rack so excess can drip off.

Place chicken on a parchment-covered sheet pan or in a lightly oiled cast-iron pan and drizzle with the remaining 2 tbsp of oil.

Roast for 30 minutes, then reduce heat to 350°F and roast for another 10 minutes.

Remove from the oven and let rest for 5–10 minutes.

This chicken is really good served at room temperature,
so it's a good one to take on a picnic.

Grilled Spanish Paella

This divine barbecued version of paella, shared with me by the wonderful Cal and Loree Renwick, is amazing. We felt so lucky to enjoy it one delightful evening at their home on the shores of Queens Bay. Their paella reminds me of being in Spain! I've loved paella since the first time I ate it while bicycling the Camino de Santiago, where so many restaurants had grills out front with aromas of seafood, chorizo and saffron in the air. I cherish this memory for the senses whenever I make this beauty here at home, whether on the grill or stovetop. SERVES 6–8

ingredients

16 large prawns, peeled
   and tails left on
2 tbsp smoked paprika
4–6 boneless, skinless chicken
   thighs, cut into 1-inch pieces
salt and freshly ground pepper
   for seasoning
4–6 dried or fresh Spanish
   chorizo sausages, cut into
   ¼-inch thick rounds
1–2 tbsp olive oil, as needed
1 medium onion, finely diced
2 medium garlic cloves,
   minced
2 tbsp paella spice
1 tsp saffron threads
2 medium ripe tomatoes,
   diced, or 1 14-oz can diced
   fire-roasted tomatoes
2 cups Spanish bomba rice,
   or any medium-grain rice
1 tsp kosher or Maldon salt
4 cups chicken broth
16 mussels, scrubbed
2 tbsp Italian parsley, chopped
2 medium lemons, cut into
   8 wedges for serving

method

Place prawns in a medium-size bowl. Add ¼ tsp of the paprika, season with salt and pepper and toss to combine. Refrigerate.

Place chicken in a medium sized bowl and season generously with salt and pepper. Set aside.

Heat an outdoor grill to high (about 450–550° F), or your stovetop burner to medium-high heat.

Place paella pan on the grill or burner, cover, and heat until hot, about 2 minutes.

Add chorizo to the pan, close the grill and cook, stirring occasionally, until chorizo is starting to brown and the fat is rendered. Remove chorizo to a large bowl and set aside.

Add 1–2 tbsp of olive oil to the pan. There should still be a thin layer of rendered fat in the pan.

Add the seasoned chicken to the pan in a single layer. Close the grill and sear or put the lid on the pan and stir occasionally, until all sides of the chicken are golden brown. Rotate the pan occasionally on the grill to evenly distribute the heat. Remove chicken to the bowl with the chorizo and set aside.

Add onion to the pan, season with salt and pepper, close the grill and cook. Stir occasionally, until onions are softened but not brown. If using the stovetop, cook the onions until soft.

Add remaining paprika, garlic, paella spice and saffron and stir to combine. Cook until fragrant, about 30 seconds.

Add tomatoes and juices. Cook until the mixture has slightly darkened in colour, scraping up any browned bits from the bottom of the pan.

Add the rice and 1 tsp salt. Stir to coat.

Add broth and stir. Arrange rice mixture in an even layer. Place chorizo and chicken evenly over rice, adding any juices from the bowl. Do not stir the rice from this point on.

Close the grill or cover with a lid and bring to a lively simmer. Maintain and check occasionally until the rice grains swell, most liquid has been absorbed and the rice begins to make a crackling sound, about 12 minutes.

Arrange the prawns and mussels (hinge-side-down) on the rice, nestling them in slightly.

Close the grill or cover with a lid. Cook until the mussels have opened, the shrimp are just cooked through and the rice is tender, but still al dente, about 10–12 minutes.

Remove the pan from the grill or stovetop and sprinkle on the chopped parsley.

Serve with the lemon wedges.

*Place some chairs around the barbecue, pour everyone some wine
and savour the process of making this lovely grilled paella. Thanks, Cal and Loree!*

Nonna's
Lasagna and Fried Chicken

Nonna Grace's daughter-in-law, Sue McLaughlin, shared this Italian classic with us for this book. Grace doesn't believe in adding any "fancy stuff." I can still hear her, "This is not lasagna!" when I made one with roasted vegetables and bechamel sauce in honour of her late husband, Izzie, but Grace did okay us adding a ricotta and spinach layer to her recipe! She serves the lasagna first, then the chicken and plain green beans or a simple salad. SERVES 8–10

ingredients

Meat Sauce

¼ cup vegetable oil
1 medium onion, diced
5 cloves garlic, minced
1½ lbs lean ground beef
2 28-oz cans or jars of your favourite tomato sauce
1 10-oz tin tomato paste
1 cup parsley, chopped
1 cup fresh basil, chopped

Ricotta Spinach Layer

475 g ricotta cheese
1 egg, beaten
½ cup parsley, chopped
2 cups spinach leaves
½ tsp nutmeg
pinch of salt and pepper

1 box lasagna noodles
2 450 g balls regular mozzarella, grated (8 cups)
2 cups Parmesan cheese, grated
6–8 whole basil leaves for garnishing

method

Meat Sauce

Place oil, onion and garlic in a large saucepan on medium heat and cook for about 5 minutes until the onions are soft.

Add the ground beef and cook for another 10–15 minutes, until liquid has evaporated.

Add tomato sauce, tomato paste, parsley and basil.

Increase heat to medium-high until it comes to a low boil. Reduce heat and simmer for 2–3 hours, stirring occasionally.

Ricotta Spinach Layer

Mix all ingredients together in a mixing bowl and set aside.

Preheat oven to 250°F.

Cook lasagna noodles according to package directions and let cool.

Fried Chicken

6–8 chicken thighs, bone in and skin on
salt and pepper
2 eggs, slightly beaten
¼ cup milk
1½ cups bread crumbs
½ cup panko
vegetable oil, quantity as required in method

Assemble Lasagna

Spread a bit of meat sauce in a 9 x 13-inch baking dish so the noodles don't stick to the bottom.

Layer noodles on top, then a generous amount of sauce followed by mozzarella and Parmesan cheese.

Place another layer of noodles and top with the spinach and ricotta mixture.

Repeat the process until the dish is full (there should be 4 layers), ending with a cheese layer.

Garnish with whole basil leaves.

Cover tightly with tin foil and bake for 2 hours.

Remove from the oven and take off the tin foil.

Broil a few minutes to brown the cheese a bit.

Fried Chicken

Salt and pepper chicken generously on both sides.

Add milk to beaten eggs in a medium-size bowl.

Combine bread crumbs and panko in another bowl.

Dip each chicken piece into egg mixture, then into crumb mixture, coating chicken on both sides.

Add oil ¼ way up the side of a large skillet and place on medium-high heat.

Fry chicken until golden brown, but not fully cooked.

Place chicken in a baking dish, cover with tinfoil and cook with the lasagna for 2 hours. Leave the tinfoil off if you want the chicken to be crispier.

You can make the lasagna ahead of time and freeze it until needed.

Korean Slow-Roasted Pork Butt
with Kimchi and Ssam Sauce

Conner made this for dinner for us one night during our COVID-19 lockdown and we screamed with every bite as the flavours just got better and better! We loved all the different sauces, pickles and the kimchi accompaniments. Make them all while the pork is roasting in the oven. You can eat the pork like lettuce wraps or just with a knife and fork on a plate, spooning all the yummy sauces onto your pork and rice. SERVES 6–8

ingredients

Pork

1 bone-in pork butt, 2.25 kg (about 5 lbs)
½ cup white sugar
½ cup plus 1 tbsp kosher salt, divided
½ cup brown sugar

Ginger Scallion Sauce

2½ cups green onions or scallions, green and white parts, thinly sliced
½ cup ginger, peeled and minced or microplaned
¼ cup vegetable oil
4 tsp soy sauce
2 tsp sherry or rice vinegar
½ tsp salt

Ssam Sauce

2 tbsp fermented bean and chili paste (ssamjang) or black bean garlic sauce
1 tbsp chili paste (gochujang)
½ cup sherry or rice wine vinegar
½ cup vegetable oil

Bailey's Quick Pickles

1 long English cucumber or 6 Persian cucumbers, cubed
3 cloves garlic, minced
2 tbsp rice wine vinegar
2 tsp sesame oil
1 tsp salt
1 tsp sugar
1 tsp sesame seeds, toasted
1 tsp red chili flakes

Accompaniments

2 cups basmati rice, cooked
2 heads butter lettuce, leaves separated, washed and dried
1–2 cups kimchi

method

Pork

Place the pork in a large shallow bowl. Mix white sugar and ½ cup of kosher salt together. Rub the mixture all over the pork. Wrap pork in plastic wrap and place in the bowl. Refrigerate for at least 6 hours or overnight.

Preheat oven to 300°F.

Remove pork from the fridge, remove plastic wrap, brush off excess sugar mixture and discard any juices from the bowl.

Place pork in a roasting pan and roast for approximately 5 hours or until it can be pulled apart with a fork. Baste the pork with the pan juices every hour.

Let pork rest for up to an hour.

Heat oven to 500°F.

Combine the remaining 1 tbsp of salt with the brown sugar and rub all over the cooked pork butt.

Roast until a dark crust forms, about 10–12 minutes and remove from the oven.

Ginger Scallion Sauce

Combine all ginger scallion sauce ingredients in a small bowl and set aside.

Ssam Sauce

Combine all ssam sauce ingredients in a small bowl and set aside.

Bailey's Quick Pickles

Combine all pickle ingredients in a small bowl and set aside.

to serve

Place cooked basmati rice in a bowl, lettuce leaves on a platter and kimchi in a small bowl.

Slice or shred the pork, place on a serving platter and drizzle with some of the ssam sauce.

Set the pork and all its accompaniments in the middle of the table and dive in!

The ssamjang, gochujang and black bean garlic sauce can be found in Nelson at Wings on Baker Street, or any large grocery store these days because Korean food is so popular. I buy my kimchi at the Kootenay Co-op because they sell locally made ones, but most stores carry it.

dinners

The Kootenay Bowl
with Ali's Perfect Salmon with Crispy Skin

This yummy bowl includes the Edamame Rice Noodle Salad with Tamarind Vinaigrette found on page 64 and is topped with Ali's perfect crispy-skinned salmon. I always like to include a complete lunch- or dinner-in-a-bowl recipe in the Whitewater cookbooks for a go-to meal that I know will always make me happy, full and healthy! SERVES 4

ingredients

Prepare the Edamame and Rice Noodle Salad with Tamarind Vinaigrette found on page 64.

8 radishes, thinly sliced
2 tbsp rice wine vinegar
2 tsp sugar
2 cups spicy greens or baby bok choy
2 tbsp sesame seeds, toasted

Ali's Perfect Salmon with Crispy Skin
2 tbsp olive oil
4 6–oz salmon fillets, skin on
salt and pepper

method

Pickle the radishes in the vinegar and sugar for at least 15 minutes.

Ali's Perfect Salmon with Crispy Skin

Heat oil over medium-high heat in a frying pan.

Sprinkle both sides of salmon with salt and pepper.

Sear salmon skin-side-down for 4 minutes.

Flip over and sear the other side for 4 minutes or less.

Remove from the pan.

Remove the skin and fry it in the same pan until crispy.

to assemble

Place the Edamame and Rice Noodle Salad in 4 bowls.

Set the salmon and crispy skin on top of the noodles.

Top with pickled radishes, greens and a sprinkle of the sesame seeds.

Another drizzle of the Tamarind Dressing and you're set! You can divide this recipe in half if there are just two of you or save the extra bowl for lunch tomorrow.

Braised Moroccan-Inspired Garlicky
Short Ribs

This comfy make-ahead dish has a very easy preparation. It's excellent served with Christy's Cauliflower and Potato Mash from *Whitewater Cooks More Beautiful Food* and Petra's Preserved Lemon and Crystallized Ginger Salad found on page 52 of this book. SERVES 6

ingredients

- 2 tbsp vegetable oil
- 5 lbs bone-in short ribs, at least 1½ inches thick
- kosher salt and pepper
- 2 large whole heads of garlic, cut in half, skin left on
- 1 medium onion, diced
- 4 ribs celery, diced
- 2 medium carrots, diced
- 2 tbsp harissa paste
- 1 tbsp tomato paste
- 1 tsp cinnamon
- 2 cups red or white wine
- 2 cups beef stock
- 4 sprigs thyme
- 2 bay leaves
- 1 cup parsley
- ½ cup green onion, finely chopped
- 1 tbsp finely grated orange zest

method

Preheat oven to 275°F.

Heat oil in a large Dutch oven over medium-high heat.

Season short ribs on all sides with salt and pepper.

Sear short ribs on all sides, in batches, until deeply browned, about 8 minutes per batch. Transfer browned short ribs to a large plate.

Pour off fat, leaving 2 tablespoons of it and the browned bits behind.

Reduce heat to medium and add garlic, cut-side-down. Cook without moving for about 2 minutes.

Add onion, celery and carrots and season with salt and pepper. Stir well and continue to cook until vegetables are soft but not browned, about 5–10 minutes.

Add harissa and tomato pastes and cinnamon and stir to coat the vegetables.

Cook for another 2–3 minutes.

Add wine, scrape up the browned bits and let simmer for 2–3 minutes.

Stir in the beef stock, thyme and bay leaves.

Place the short ribs in the pan, using tongs to immerse them bone-side-up. Pour in any juices from the plate they were resting on. Add more stock or water if needed to cover the ribs.

Bring to a simmer, then cover with a lid and place in the oven.

Cook undisturbed until the meat is tender and almost falling off the bone, about 3½–4 hours.

Remove the ribs from the pot using tongs, trying to keep the bones in place. Set them on a large platter to rest.

Strain the sauce into a bowl or large glass measuring cup and skim off some of the fat. Throw away the cooking vegetables and herbs, but save the garlic.

Put the ribs back in the pot with the garlic and the strained sauce.

Scatter the parsley, green onions and orange zest over the ribs.

You could serve these ribs right out of the pot with the veggies and garlic still in there. It's equally as spectacular as plating them, but just a little more rustic.

Mike's Famous
Duck Salad Dinner

One night when I was away Mike really wanted to eat some duck and this is what he made. We love it and it's become his "famous" duck salad recipe! It's not quite filling enough for us big eaters, so we often have it with a baguette and cheese. SERVES 2

ingredients

Vinaigrette

2 tbsp red wine vinegar
1 tsp Dijon mustard
½ tsp dried or fresh tarragon
½ tsp pepper
½ tsp salt, more to taste
1 tbsp parsley, finely chopped
3 tbsp olive oil

Salad

2 boneless duck breasts
salt and pepper
4 strips thick bacon
1 small head romaine lettuce, chopped
2 apples, thinly sliced
½ cup dried cranberries, soaked in warm water for 5 minutes to soften
2 large shallots, thinly sliced and fried in oil until crisp (optional but delicious!)

method

Vinaigrette

Combine vinaigrette ingredients and whisk until well combined. Set aside.

Salad

Score the duck skin and fat in a criss-cross pattern, being careful not to pierce the meat.
Season the duck breasts with salt and pepper and set aside.
Cook the bacon until crispy, about 8 minutes, and drain it on paper towels. Crumble the bacon and set aside.
Preheat oven to 400°F.
Place the duck breasts skin-side-down in a cold cast-iron pan and turn the heat to medium-high.
Cook until the skin is crispy and golden, about 10 minutes, reducing heat as needed to prevent splattering.
Flip and sear for 1 minute, transfer the pan to the oven and roast until cooked to your liking (about 4 minutes for medium and 7 minutes for medium well).
Remove the pan from the oven and set the duck breasts aside to rest while you prepare the rest of the salad.
Re-stir the vinaigrette, then toss it with the lettuce.
Divide the lettuce among serving bowls or plates and top with the bacon, sliced apple and cranberries.
Slice the duck breasts thinly and distribute the pieces onto the salads.
Top with crispy shallots if using.

Sometimes if we have leftover Scalloped Potatoes Gratin (page 88), we reheat it to serve with this beautiful light dinner salad.

Brown Butter Scallop Risotto
with Garlicky Kale, Preserved Lemon and Crispy Sage Leaves

This bowl of goodness is just the right decadent dinner for a romantic date or when you need to feel pampered.
Make the risotto first, then the kale, brown butter, and crispy sage leaves, saving the scallops for last so they're super fresh! SERVES 4

ingredients

Risotto

4   cups chicken stock
1   tbsp butter
1   garlic clove, minced
1   shallot, minced
1   cup arborio rice
½   cup white wine
½   cup Parmesan
salt and pepper to taste

Garlicky Kale

1   tbsp olive oil
2   garlic cloves, thinly sliced
4   cups kale or spinach,
    torn into bite-size pieces

Brown Butter

4   tbsp butter

Garnish

12 sage leaves
2   tbsp olive oil
1   tbsp preserved lemon,
    finely chopped

Scallops

1   lb large scallops
salt
1   tbsp vegetable oil

method

Risotto

Place the chicken stock in a saucepan and heat until just barely simmering.

Melt the butter over medium heat in a large non-stick pan or wok.

Add the garlic and shallot and sauté for a minute or two until soft.

Add rice and stir until coated with the butter.

Add the white wine and let it sizzle for a bit. Stir until absorbed into the rice.

Ladle in the warm chicken stock, ½ cup at a time, and cook over a lively simmer, stirring after each addition until absorbed into the rice. Continue until the rice is soft and creamy, but al dente.

Add more stock if you like your risotto creamier.

Turn off the heat.

Add the Parmesan and mix until combined.

Sprinkle with salt and pepper to taste and cover.

Garlicky Kale

Heat the olive oil over medium-low heat.

Add the garlic and cook for a minute until a bit crispy.

Add the kale or spinach and cook until wilted. Turn off heat.

Brown Butter

Place the butter in a small saucepan over medium heat and stir until golden and foamy, about 5 minutes.

Turn off heat.

Garnish

Sauté whole sage leaves in olive oil until just crisp, about 30 seconds. Drain on paper towels.

Scallops

Pat the scallops dry with paper towels.

Sprinkle with a little bit of salt.

Heat the oil in a large frying pan over medium-high until hot.

Add scallops and cook 2–3 minutes per side until golden brown and opaque in the centre.

Transfer to a plate and cover gently until needed.

to assemble

Divide risotto among four bowls or plates.

Place scallops and kale on top and drizzle with the brown butter.

Garnish with crispy sage leaves and chopped preserved lemon if desired.

A squeeze of fresh lemon would be really good too!
Prawns would also be amazing with this risotto if scallops aren't your thing.

Sweet
Steelhead

Steelhead is definitely one of my favourite fish. In flavour it's a combination of salmon and trout, and it's oily like sablefish, which really makes for a perfect fish. The talented chef Alivia shared this unique and totally flavourful steelhead recipe.

SERVES 4

ingredients

4 6-oz steelhead fillets
2 tbsp dark brown sugar
1 tsp cinnamon
1 tsp sumac
½ tsp paprika
¼ tsp salt
1 orange, zest
Maldon salt
1 blood orange, thinly sliced
   for garnish, if available

method

Preheat oven to 400°F.

Lay fillets on a baking tray lined with parchment paper.

Mix together brown sugar, cinnamon, sumac, paprika, salt and orange zest in a small bowl, making sure everything is well incorporated.

Rub mixture onto fillets, making sure fish is evenly coated.

Roast until the fish flakes easily when pricked with a fork, 15–20 minutes.

Sprinkle with a little Maldon salt before serving to balance out the sweet and fat components.

Top with thinly sliced blood orange for a beautiful presentation.

The Roasted Sumac Veggies (page 78) and Gail's Coconut Rice (page 99)
pair really well with this yummy fish.

Gochujang
Chicken

I love the flavour gochujang gives to a slow-roasted chicken. Gochujang is a Korean hot chili paste that's packed with flavour. The slow roasting of this chicken and potatoes reminds me of a street market where the chickens are roasting on a rotisserie and the fat is dripping down over the little potatoes below. SERVES 4

ingredients

1   3½–4 lb chicken
1   tbsp Maldon or kosher salt
freshly ground black pepper
½   cup gochujang paste
¼   cup plus 2 tbsp olive oil,
      divided
2   whole heads garlic, halved
2   tbsp ginger, peeled
      and grated
1½ lbs baby potatoes
5   green onions, thinly sliced
2   tsp honey
2–3 limes, 1 for squeezing
      and the rest cut into wedges
cilantro sprigs for garnishing

method

Preheat oven to 300°F
Pat chicken dry with paper towels and place on a baking sheet. Season all over with salt and pepper, including inside the cavity.
Mix gochujang, 1/4 cup oil, 3 garlic cloves (minced) and ginger in a small bowl.
Put the remainder of the first garlic head inside the chicken cavity. Tie legs together with kitchen twine.
Coat the whole chicken with half of the gochujang mixture using a pastry brush.

Place the potatoes and the second garlic head in a mixing bowl and add the remaining gochujang mixture and the 2 tbsp olive oil. Season lightly with salt and pepper and combine well.
Place potatoes around the outside of a large cast-iron pan, leaving room for the chicken.
Arrange garlic halves cut-side-down in the middle of the pan. Set chicken on top.
Roast chicken and potatoes for 2 ½–3 hours, turning the potatoes over a few times to coat in the juices.

Transfer chicken to a cutting board. Let rest at least 15 minutes.
Stir honey and juice of half of 1 lime into potatoes. Sprinkle with green onions.
Carve chicken and place the pieces over potatoes.
Squeeze remaining lime half over the chicken.
Garnish with lime wedges and cilantro sprigs.

Bailey's Quick Pickles (page 128) are a refreshing accompaniment for this spicy chicken!

desserts

Italian Nonna
Ricotta Cake

Only a true Italian nonna could produce a cake with such a simple list of ingredients.
It's light and airy but also rich and flavourful. It would be delicious with some stewed rhubarb or fresh raspberries. SERVES 6

ingredients

9   tbsp unsalted butter,
    room temperature
1   cup plus 2 tbsp sugar
3   large eggs, room temperature
1¼ cups all-purpose flour
1   tbsp baking powder
¼   tsp salt
1   cup ricotta cheese
1   lemon, zest
1   apple, peeled and grated
    (about 1 cup)
icing sugar for serving

method

Preheat oven to 400°F.

Butter and flour a 9- or 10-inch springform pan.

Cream butter and sugar until light and fluffy using a hand mixer,
about 5–8 minutes.

Add eggs 1 at a time, mixing until just combined.

Fold in the flour, baking powder, salt, ricotta, lemon zest, and apple.

Scrape the batter into the prepared pan and smooth the top with a spatula.

Bake for 30–35 minutes until the cake is golden brown and the sides
start to pull away from the pan.

Cool in the pan on a wire rack for 10 minutes.

Turn the cake out of the pan and cool completely on the rack.

Sift the icing sugar over the top of the cake before serving.

I love this simple cake! It would be great for breakfast with a really good espresso.

Buttermilk Vanilla Bean Panna Cotta
with Boozy Berries

Thanks, Emmy, for sharing this unique panna cotta recipe. I love the flavour of the buttermilk and vanilla bean together. Yum!

SERVES 6

ingredients

Buttermilk Vanilla Bean Panna Cotta

1½ tsp unflavoured gelatin

1¼ cups whipping cream

7 tbsp sugar

½ vanilla bean pod,
split lengthwise and scraped

1¾ cups full-fat buttermilk

Boozy Blackberries

3 cups blackberries

2 tbsp sugar

1 tbsp Grand Marnier
or liqueur of choice
(optional)

method

Buttermilk Vanilla Bean Panna Cotta

Soften the gelatin in 1 tbsp cold water in a medium-size bowl.

Heat cream and sugar together in a small saucepan over medium heat.

Add vanilla seeds and pod to cream mixture.

Stir until sugar dissolves, 3–5 minutes.

Add warm cream mixture to gelatin and stir until well incorporated and gelatin is totally dissolved.

Add buttermilk and stir again, mixing thoroughly.

Strain mixture into a medium-size pitcher.

Divide mixture among 6 ramekins or pretty wine glasses.

Refrigerate at least 4 hours until set.

Boozy Blackberries

Mash 1 cup of the berries and then strain out the juice. Discard seeds.

Place juice in a small saucepan and add sugar. Heat over low heat, stirring to dissolve sugar, and reduce until slightly thickened, about 2 minutes.

Top the panna cotta with a spoonful of the cooled, thickened juice and the remaining berries. Drizzle with Grand Marnier, if using.

I like to use blackberries if they're in season, but raspberries and strawberries are yummy too.
Panna cotta means "cooked cream" in Italian. Prego!

Easy-Peasy
Hazelnut Torte

Claire Hitchman is the most adorable human on the planet Earth! She has been making this cake since she was in her early twenties, when no one owned an electric mixer but we all had blenders for making margaritas, of course! SERVES 6–8

ingredients

Torte

6 eggs
1½ cups ground hazelnuts
1⅛ cups white sugar
3 tbsp flour
3¼ tsp baking powder

Whipped Cream Frosting

2 cups whipping cream
1 cup white sugar
4 tsp vanilla
1 cup good quality dark cocoa, sifted

method

Torte

Preheat oven to 350°F.

Butter and flour two 9-inch cake tins.

Combine eggs, hazelnuts and sugar in a blender or food processor and blend at high speed for about 1 minute.

Add flour and baking powder and blend only until combined.

Divide batter into prepared cake pans and bake for 20 minutes.

Cool slightly and turn out onto a rack to cool to room temperature.

Whipped Cream Frosting

Whip the cream until stiff peaks form.

Fold in sugar, vanilla and cocoa.

Spread ⅓ of the frosting on one of the cooled cakes.

Top with the other layer and spread remaining frosting all over the top and sides of the cake.

Top with broken-up Ferraro Rocher chocolates and raspberries for a really fun presentation if you like!

Apricot Kuchen
with Labneh Whipped Cream

This kuchen is, of course, best with fresh apricots, but we discovered that using canned or preserved apricots in the winter works just as well. I was almost not going to include this recipe because we had to do the photo shoot when apricots weren't in season, but I'm so glad I did! SERVES 8

ingredients

Apricot Kuchen

1¼ cups all-purpose flour
½ cup sugar
    plus 1 tbsp for sprinkling
1 tbsp cornmeal
2 tsp baking powder
¼ tsp sea salt
½ cup unsalted butter,
    room temperature
1 large egg, lightly beaten
½ tsp almond extract
1 lb fresh apricots, cut in half
    (about 8–10 small
    or 6 medium)

Labneh Whipped Cream

⅔ cup whipping cream
½ cup labneh or full-fat
    Greek yogurt
1 tbsp icing sugar

method

Apricot Kuchen

Preheat oven to 350°F.

Spray a 9-inch tart pan with cooking spray or rub with soft butter.

Place flour, sugar, cornmeal, baking powder and salt into a bowl and combine well with a whisk.

Add butter and beat until mostly incorporated using electric beaters or a standing mixer.

Add egg and almond extract and beat until ingredients are completely incorporated and dough forms a ball, about 30 seconds.

Gather dough from bowl.

Press about 1¼ cups dough into the pan, pressing evenly onto the bottom and up the fluted sides.

Wrap remaining dough. Place the pan and wrapped dough in the refrigerator for at least ½ hour.

Arrange apricots cut-side-up on the chilled tart pan dough, leaving a bit of room in between them (you may need more or fewer apricots).

Tear remaining dough into pieces and tuck between apricots.

Sprinkle with 1 tbsp sugar.

Bake until crisp and golden, about 45 minutes.

Transfer to a wire rack and let cool for 30 minutes before removing from the pan.

Labneh Whipped Cream

Beat cream until soft peaks form, about 1 minute.

Add labneh and icing sugar and beat until just combined.

to serve

Slice kuchen and serve with labneh whipped cream.

You could also use peaches or plums in this versatile kuchen.

Fudgy
Coconut Oat Bars

These bars are perfect at 3 p.m. with your afternoon latte. Thanks to the lovely Linda for sharing these yummy treats.

MAKES 24–36 BARS

ingredients

Fudgy Topping

2   195 ml cans organic sweetened
    condensed coconut milk
14 oz dark chocolate, finely chopped
    (2½ cups)
1   tbsp almond butter
    (or cashew butter)
½   cup slivered almonds and/
    or coconut ribbons

Oat Bars

1   cup butter
¼   cup almond butter
    (cashew butter is good too)
1⅓ cups cane or regular white sugar
2   eggs, room temperature
2   cups rolled oats
2   cups all-purpose flour
1   tsp baking soda
pinch of salt

method

Fudgy Topping

Combine condensed coconut milk, dark chocolate and
1 tbsp nut butter in a saucepan over medium heat.
Stir until chocolate is melted and mixture is smooth.

Oat Bars

Preheat oven to 350°F.
Beat butter, nut butter and sugar until creamy.
Add eggs 1 at a time while beating.
Mix together dry ingredients and add to the wet.
Reserve a healthy 1 cup of the batter for topping.
Spread the remainder into a parchment-lined 9 x 13-inch pan.
Pour fudgy topping over the batter.
Drop reserved oat mixture over top in little dollops and
sprinkle with almonds and/or coconut ribbons.
Bake for 25 minutes until the topping is golden brown.
Cool completely and cut into desired size.
They're pretty rich so a smaller bar is perfect.

*These bars are also fabulous to take along as a hiking or ski touring snack
to reward you in the middle or at the end of your adventure.*

Lemon Velvet
Sheet Cake

A beautiful, simple, light and fresh cake that we all need to have in our go-to repertoires! It can be dolled up with whipped cream and toasted coconut ribbons for a party cake or served straight-up with its lemon glaze to enjoy with a cup of afternoon tea.

SERVES 6–8

ingredients

Cake

1½ cups cake flour
1½ cups all-purpose flour
2 tsp baking powder
¼ tsp baking soda
¾ tsp salt
2 cups sugar
¼ cup packed lemon zest
   (about 4 lemons)
¾ cup vegetable oil
1 tsp lemon extract (optional)
½ tsp vanilla extract
2 large eggs, room temperature
2 large egg yolks,
   room temperature
¼ cup lemon juice
1 cup crème fraîche or
   sour cream

Glaze

2½ cups icing sugar, sifted
5 tbsp freshly squeezed lemon
   juice (about 1 large lemon)

method

Cake

Preheat oven to 350°F.

Grease a 9 x 13-inch pan with butter and line with parchment paper.

Put both flours, baking powder, baking soda and salt in a medium-size bowl and whisk until well combined.

Place sugar and lemon zest in a large bowl and rub together to infuse the flavour.

Whisk in the oil and the extracts until smooth.

Whisk in eggs and yolks until fully incorporated.

Add lemon juice and whisk again, then crème fraîche or sour cream, whisking vigorously.

Add dry ingredients all at once, gently folding with a spatula until just incorporated.

Transfer batter to prepared pan and bake for 30–35 minutes, until cake is golden and firm to the touch.

Let the cake cool for 15 minutes in the pan, then turn out onto a cooling rack and then invert it so the top side is up on the cooling rack.

Glaze

Whisk the icing sugar and lemon juice together until smooth.

Pour evenly over the cake. If the glaze pools, smooth with a spatula. You can also leave the cake in the pan and glaze it there.

A cup of mashed fresh or frozen raspberries mixed into some whipped cream turns this cake into a fun kid's birthday cake!

Spicy Chocolate
Hazelnut Cookies

The flavour of these cookies reminds me of Nutella! The combo of hazelnuts and chocolate is always so addictive. The addition of black pepper and crystallized ginger makes them really unusual and so yummy. MAKES 12 COOKIES

ingredients

2 cups hazelnut flour
   or finely ground hazelnuts
1 cup packed brown sugar
1½ tsp baking powder
½ tsp baking soda
1 tsp freshly ground black pepper
¼ tsp salt
1 large egg, lightly beaten
2 tbsp unsalted butter, melted
1 tsp hazelnut or vanilla extract
½ cup bittersweet chocolate,
   chopped into little pieces
⅓ cup crystallized ginger,
   chopped into little pieces

method

Whisk together the hazelnut flour, brown sugar, baking powder, baking soda, black pepper and salt in a large mixing bowl.

Add the egg, melted butter, hazelnut extract, chocolate and ginger.

Stir with a large wooden spoon until the dough comes together.

Grease your hands with a little oil to prevent dough from sticking and divide it into 12 equal parts (approximately ¼ cup each).

Shape them into balls.

Flatten them into 2-inch rounds.

Place the rounds on a parchment-lined baking sheet and wrap the entire sheet in plastic wrap.

Place in the freezer for at least 30 minutes and preferably 2 hours.

Preheat the oven to 350°F.

Remove cookies from the freezer and bake for 12–15 minutes.

Cool completely on wire racks.

If you can't find hazelnut flour, almond flour works well too.
If you'd like a spicier cookie, double the black pepper!

Triple
Coconut Cream Pie

I absolutely love coconut cream pie! This recipe was shared by the amazing baker and my precious friend Emmy McKnight.
It's a bit of a project, but worth every step! SERVES 8

ingredients

Dough

1 cup plus 2 tbsp
  all-purpose flour
½ cup sweetened
  shredded coconut
½ cup cold unsalted butter,
  cut into ½-inch cubes
2 tsp sugar
¼ tsp salt
⅓ cup ice water

Pastry Cream

1 cup milk
1 cup canned unsweetened
  coconut milk, stirred
2 cups shredded
  sweetened coconut
1 vanilla bean, split and
  seeds scraped out
2 large eggs
½ cup plus 2 tbsp sugar
3 tbsp flour
4 tbsp unsalted butter, cubed,
  room temperature

Topping

1½ cups unsweetened
  large shred coconut or
  coconut ribbons
2½ cups whipping cream, chilled
⅓ cup sugar
1 tsp vanilla extract
2 oz white chocolate, shaved

method

Dough

Put all dough ingredients except ice water into a food processor and pulse until coarse crumbs form.

Gradually add 1 tablespoon of ice water at a time, pulsing after each addition, until dough just holds together when you pinch it between your fingers. The dough will be quite loose.

Gather dough and pile onto a piece of plastic wrap.

Press the dough into a round flattened disc. Wrap in plastic wrap and chill for at least ½ hour or more.

Preheat the oven to 400°F.

Unwrap dough and place on a lightly floured surface.

Roll out dough into a large circle, about 12 inches.

Transfer dough to a 9-inch pie pan, being careful not to stretch it.

Trim any excess to allow for a 1-inch overhang. Turn edges neatly over and crimp evenly along the rim.

Prick pastry with a fork.

Place a piece of parchment into the pie shell and fill with pie weights or beans to prevent the crust from puffing up during baking.

Bake the crust until the pastry rim is golden, about 20 minutes. Remove weights from shell and return to oven until the bottom of the crust is golden, about another 10–12 minutes.

Remove from oven and allow to cool.

*Phew! Now that you've made this luscious pie,
sit down and savour every mouthful — you deserve it!*

Pastry Cream

Combine milk, coconut milk, coconut, vanilla seeds and pod in a medium saucepan. Heat until almost to a boil.

Whisk eggs, sugar and flour together in a medium bowl until well combined.

Pour a small amount of the hot milk slowly into the egg mixture while whisking.

Add egg and milk mixture back to milk mixture. Whisk until it begins to bubble and is very thick. Do not let it stick to the pot's bottom.

Remove vanilla pod and transfer the pastry cream to a bowl. Whisk in the butter cube by cube until it melts.

Set bowl in an ice bath, stirring occasionally until cooled.

Cover surface with plastic wrap to prevent a skin forming. Refrigerate until completely cold.

Fill pie shell with pastry cream and smooth.

Topping

Preheat oven to 350°F.

Toast coconut about 5 minutes until it starts to brown. Watch carefully as it burns easily.

Whip cream, sugar and vanilla to firm peaks.

Fill a pastry bag with a star tip with cream. Pipe onto pastry cream or mound it on.

Garnish pie with toasted coconut and shaved white chocolate.

Pumpkin
Olive Oil Loaf

Conner used to stop at his favourite little coffee place in Brooklyn on his way to work and have a big slice of this delicious loaf. Especially after this year of not being able to travel anywhere, eating something delicious and pretending we're somewhere else is important! MAKES 2 9 x 5-inch loaves

ingredients

3½ cups all-purpose flour
2 tsp baking soda
1½ tsp salt
1 tsp ground nutmeg
1 tsp ground cinnamon
1 tsp ground cloves
1 tsp ground ginger
½ cup unsalted butter
3 cups sugar
2 cups pumpkin purée
⅔ cup water
½ cup olive oil
4 large eggs, room temperature
⅓ cup raw pumpkin seeds
⅓ cup turbinado sugar (optional)

method

Preheat oven to 350°F.

Grease two 9 x 5-inch loaf pans with soft butter and dust with flour.

Combine the flour, baking soda, salt and all the spices in a medium-size mixing bowl and set aside.

Melt butter in a small saucepan over low heat and set aside to cool.

Blend the sugar, pumpkin purée, water, olive oil and melted butter in a mixing bowl using an electric beater, until smooth.

Add the eggs 1 at a time with the mixer on medium-low and mix until well combined.

Add the flour mixture in 3 batches, mixing on low speed to combine between additions.

After the third addition, mix for 15 seconds to ensure the batter is smooth.

Split the batter evenly between the 2 prepared loaf pans.

Top with the pumpkin seeds and turbinado sugar if using.

Bake for 55–60 minutes or until a toothpick or skewer inserted in the centre of the loaf comes out clean.

Let cool on a baking rack for 10 minutes, then flip out of the pans.

*You could, of course, add a cup of chocolate chips
to one or both of these loaves for a sweeter treat.*

Paul's Mom's Classic
Buttermilk Bran Muffins

Paul's mom, Marjorie, is the sweetest gal you have ever met. We've been making her moist and healthy muffins for years and I'm not sure why I haven't shared them in the *Whitewater Cooks* books until now. Thanks, Paul and Gail, for reminding us about these treasured muffins. A slice of blood orange, a date or a banana slice on top before baking is essential for prettiness! MAKES 12 MUFFINS

ingredients

1   cup dates, well chopped
½   cup brown sugar
1   tsp salt
1   tsp vanilla extract
2   tbsp molasses
1   egg
¼   cup raisins, soaked in hot
     water until soft, then drained
1   tsp orange zest
1   tbsp butter, melted
1½ cups bran
1   cup flour
1   tsp baking soda
½   tsp cinnamon
½   tsp nutmeg
⅓   cup walnuts, chopped
1   cup buttermilk

method

Preheat oven to 350°F.

Place the dates in a small saucepan and cover with water.

Bring to a boil and then remove from heat and drain.
Mixture should be very soft, like a paste.

Transfer to a medium-size bowl and add brown sugar, salt, vanilla, molasses, egg, raisins, orange zest and butter. Mix until combined.

Mix the bran, flour, baking soda, spices and walnuts together in a separate bowl.

Add the date mixture and stir with a wooden spoon. The mixture will be quite dry.

Add the buttermilk and mix gently.

Scoop out into well-greased muffin tins or use muffin liners.

Let sit for 3 minutes.

Bake for 15–20 minutes.

I like to eat these dense and moist muffins with a thick slice of aged cheddar cheese.
Feel free to double this recipe if you want a bigger batch!

The Best Ever
Chocolate Banana Bread

This very dense but moist loaf is more like cake than bread, but we don't want to feel guilty about eating it for breakfast, so let's not ever call it cake! MAKES 1 LOAF

ingredients

½ cup demerara sugar

1½ cups all-purpose flour

½ cup unsweetened
   cocoa powder

1 tsp baking soda

1 tsp salt

6 tbsp unsalted butter,
   room temperature

⅓ cup granulated sugar

¼ cup light brown sugar,
   lightly packed

1 tsp vanilla extract

1 large egg

5 very ripe bananas,
   4 coarsely mashed,
   1 halved lengthwise

½ cup mascarpone cheese,
   plain full-fat yogurt
   or sour cream

method

Preheat oven to 350°F.

Spray a 9 x 5-inch loaf pan with non-stick spray or rub with butter.

Sugar the inside of the pan with ¼ cup demerara sugar, tapping out any excess.

Whisk the flour, cocoa powder, baking soda and salt together in a medium bowl.

Beat the butter, granulated sugar, light brown sugar and vanilla extract in a medium bowl with an electric mixer on high speed until very light and fluffy, 3–5 minutes.

Scrape down the sides of the bowl, add the egg and beat until well combined and the batter is light and fluffy again, about 2 more minutes.

Reduce mixer speed to low and slowly add the dry ingredients, beating until just blended.

Fold in the mashed bananas with a spatula, followed by the mascarpone cheese, mixing just to blend.

Pour the batter into the prepared loaf pan, smoothing the top.

Place the banana halves cut-side-up on top of the batter.

Sprinkle with the remaining ¼ cup demerara sugar and bake until the sides start to pull away and the bread is baked through in the centre, approximately 1½ hours and up to 10 minutes more.

Cool completely before slicing.

*This "not cake" could also be a dessert served with
a little whipped cream or your favourite vanilla ice cream.*

Peanut Butter
Bars

I used to make these bars for my kids when they were little and they loved them. Who doesn't love the combination of peanut butter and chocolate? Whoever invented Reese's Peanut Butter Cups knew what they were doing! We changed the original recipe, removing some of the icing sugar and replacing it with shredded coconut to make them even yummier.

MAKES ABOUT 16–20 BARS, depending on the size you prefer

ingredients

2¼ cups unsweetened
   shredded coconut
1½ cups icing sugar
1 tsp salt
½ cup melted butter
   (slightly cooled)
2 cups natural creamy peanut
   butter, room temperature
1 tsp vanilla extract
2 cups good quality dark
   chocolate, chopped into little
   chunks (or chocolate chips)

method

Place the coconut in a food processor and pulse a few times to finely chop.

Add icing sugar and salt and process until thoroughly mixed and finely ground.

Add melted butter, peanut butter and vanilla and process until smooth.

Place mixture in a greased 9 x 13-inch pan lined with parchment paper.

Refrigerate until firm to the touch, about an hour.

Melt chocolate in a glass bowl in the microwave.

Pour melted chocolate over the cooled peanut butter layer, smoothing with an offset or rubber spatula.

Refrigerate until chocolate is just set, about 20 minutes.

Mark into bars with a hot, dry knife, just through the chocolate layer.

Return to the fridge for at least 30 minutes before slicing.

Slice all the way with a hot, dry knife to create bars once totally set.

These bars are best stored in and eaten right out of the fridge!

Little Individual
Rustic Fruit Tarts

Bev Grimshaw shared her idea of making little individual fruit galettes with me and I loved it! Claire and I adapted the recipe, adding the frangipane and our favourite cornmeal crust. They're true little treasures, just like Bev and Claire! MAKES **8** TARTS

ingredients

4 cups fresh berries
(blueberries, strawberries,
cherries or blackberries)

Cornmeal Dough

¼ cup sour cream
¼ cup ice water
1 cup flour
⅓ cup cornmeal
2 tbsp sugar
½ tsp salt
½ cup cold unsalted butter,
cut into little cubes
1 egg, beaten
turbinado or white sugar,
for sprinkling

Frangipane

1 tbsp unsalted butter,
room temperature
¼ cup sugar
1 large egg,
room temperature
⅔ cup almond flour or
toasted ground almonds
1 tbsp all-purpose flour
1 tsp pure almond extract
pinch of salt

method

Cornmeal Dough

Stir the sour cream and ice water together in a small bowl.

Put the flour, cornmeal, sugar and salt into a mixing bowl and stir with a whisk.

Add the cold butter cubes and work into the dry ingredients with a pastry blender or your fingers until you have a nice crumbly mixture.

Add the sour cream and ice water mixture all at once to the dry ingredients. Mix together with your fingers until you can form a loose ball. It will be quite moist. Use a dusting of flour to prevent it from sticking to the counter and turn the dough out onto it.

Divide into 2 even discs, wrap and chill for at least 2 hours or overnight.

Frangipane

Combine all frangipane ingredients in a medium-size bowl and mix until smooth.

Refrigerate until ready to use.

to assemble

Remove pastry from the fridge and divide each disc into 4 equal pieces.

Roll each piece out into a 6½-inch round and place them onto 2 large baking sheets.

Spread each round with a thin layer of frangipane, leaving a 1–1½ inch border.

Pile about ½ cup berries on top of the frangipane.

Fold in the edges of the pastry and squeeze a bit to hold it together.

Brush the pastry with beaten egg and sprinkle with turbinado or white sugar.

Return to fridge for at least 30 minutes before baking.

Preheat oven to 375°F.

Bake for about 30 minutes until crust is golden brown.

Transfer to a cooling rack and let tarts cool.

Serve with whipped cream if desired.

This amount of dough, frangipane and berries can also be turned into one large tart by using a 9-inch tart pan.

desserts

The Only Cake
My Mom Ever Made

I remember this cake with such happiness. It really is the only cake my Mom ever made. She would place it on a beautiful pottery plate, shake some sifted icing sugar all over it and fill the centre with holly, hydrangea and baby's breath, but we recommend using edible flowers or fruit instead. I made it today and filled the centre with forget-me-nots. I'll never forget my Mom or this cake. SERVES 6–8

ingredients

- 1 package yellow cake mix
- 1 package vanilla instant pudding mix
- 1 cup olive oil
- 1 cup sherry
- 4 eggs, room temperature, slightly mixed

icing sugar for dusting

method

Preheat oven to 350°F.

Grease an angel food cake or bundt pan with butter, then flour it.

Stir to combine all cake ingredients in a large mixing bowl, using an electric mixer on low speed, about 30 seconds.

Then blend on medium speed until well incorporated, about 2 minutes.

Pour into the prepared pan.

Bake for 40–45 minutes.

Let cool for 10 minutes, then invert onto a cooling rack.

Place on a serving plate and dust with icing sugar.

Decorate with one of your favourite pretty things!

I was reluctant to include this recipe because of the cake and pudding mixes, but I've loved this cake my whole life and maybe you will too!

Butterscotch
Budino

This is a really popular dessert in California right now. It's basically fancy butterscotch pudding kicked up a notch.
We all loved that as kids, right? SERVES 6

ingredients

Pudding

3 cups whipping cream
1½ cups milk
1 cup plus
   2 tbsp dark brown sugar
½ cup water
1½ tsp kosher salt
1 large egg, room temperature
3 large egg yolks,
   room temperature
5 tbsp cornstarch
5 tbsp unsalted butter
1½ tbsp dark rum

Topping

1 cup whipping cream
¼ cup coconut ribbons,
   toasted (optional)
¼ cup dark rum (optional)
Maldon sea salt for garnishing

method

Pudding

Mix cream and milk together in a mixing bowl.

Place brown sugar, water and salt together in a heavy-bottomed pot and stir to combine.

Cook on medium-high heat until sugar is melted, dark brown and smells caramelized, about 10–12 minutes.

Whisk in the cream mixture until smooth, being careful as this will boil up and release steam.

Bring the mixture to a boil, then lower heat.

Place the egg, yolks and cornstarch in a medium bowl and whisk until smooth.

Whisk in 1 cup of slightly cooled butterscotch mixture until incorporated.

Transfer the egg mixture back to the pot and simmer until thickened, about 2 minutes, stirring constantly.

Remove from heat and whisk in butter and rum.

Pour pudding through a fine-mesh strainer to remove any lumps.

Divide among 6 ramekins or wine glasses.

Allow to cool for several hours.

Topping

Whip cream until thickened, about 30 seconds to 1 minute.

Top each pudding with a little bit of whipping cream, toasted coconut ribbons, a dash of rum and a few flakes of Maldon salt.

Sometimes I like to serve this dessert in a small mason jar, as follows. Make a cookie-crumb mixture of 1 cup chocolate crumbs, 2 tbsp melted butter and a pinch of salt. Divide evenly among 8 mason jars, pressing into the bottoms. Then pour slightly cooled pudding mix into the jars and refrigerate. And if you're really feeling ambitious, you could top the pudding with a layer of caramel!

Amazing
Chocolate Almond Cake

There are so many gluten-free members of our family and friends groups these days, that it really is important to have an amazing flourless chocolate cake in our back pocket. We need to satisfy everyone when it comes time to blow out the candles or have a sweet slice of cake with a cup of tea in the afternoon. SERVES 6–8

ingredients

- 4   eggs, room temperature
- 5½ oz (160 g) good quality dark chocolate
- 7   tbsp unsalted butter
- ⅓   cup cocoa powder, sifted, plus 2 tbsp for dusting
- ⅓   cup hot water
- 1⅓ cups light brown sugar, firmly packed
- 1   cup ground almonds or almond flour

method

Preheat oven to 325°F.

Grease a 10-inch round cake pan and line sides and bottom with parchment paper.

Separate eggs, being careful not to contaminate egg whites with any bits of yolk.

Cut chocolate into small pieces with a serrated knife.

Place chocolate and butter in a small saucepan.

Stir over low heat until smooth.

Remove from heat.

Blend ⅓ cup sifted cocoa powder and hot water together in a large mixing bowl, whisking until smooth.

Whisk in melted chocolate mixture, sugar, egg yolks and ground almonds until combined.

Beat egg whites with an electric mixer until soft peaks form.

Fold whites into chocolate mixture in 2 batches, gently incorporating them.

Pour the batter into the pan and place in the oven.

Bake for about 45 minutes and let cool in the pan. Remove from the pan and dust with 2 tbsp cocoa powder.

Cut with a hot, dry knife.

I like to serve this cake with a blackberry or raspberry coulis and garnish with some whole berries, but straight-up is totally fine! A dollop of whipped cream spiked with ½ tsp of espresso powder will give it a little mocha twist for those who wish!

grocaries ♡

eggplant
zucchini
raspberries
fennel
corn
parmesan
apricots
sage
lemons
corn

Index

starters

salads

soups & sides

dinners

desserts

❧ let's talk pantry ❧

CREATING MEALS from what I have on hand has always been my favourite thing to do. It's satisfying and fun, and takes the pressure off the planning and shopping part of meal preparation. Of course, having all my favourite recipes handy in my *Whitewater Cooks* cookbooks really helps too! I try to keep great ingredients in my freezer, fridge and pantry at all times. In the summer, the pantry extends to the garden, with a variety of lettuce, kale, edible flowers, and herbs. Here are some pantry items that I always keep stocked up.

in the freezer

Sablefish	Baguettes	A bin of assorted
Salmon	Bread crumbs	toasted and raw
Ahi tuna	Filo pastry	nuts and seeds:
Prawns	Puff pastry	pine nuts
Pork tenderloin	Corn tortillas	hazelnuts almonds
Ground lamb	Vanilla ice cream	walnuts
Chicken thighs	Thai spices	pistachios
Rib-eye steaks	Lime leaves	pumpkin seeds
Italian sausage	Chipotle peppers	sesame seeds
	in adobo sauce	

in the fridge

Sweet chili sauce	Fish sauce	Miso
Gochujang paste	Hoisin sauce	Tahini
Sambal oelek or	Mayonnaise	Sesame oil
a hot chili paste	Dijon mustard	Tamari
Sriracha	Horseradish	Anchovies
chili sauce	Kalamata and	Fig jam
Curry paste	gremolata olives	Cheese: Parmesan,
Yuzu kosho	Capers	feta, sharp cheddar
Wasabi paste	Pickles	and Manchego
Basil and lemongrass	Sushi ginger	Barbecue sauce
pastes	Preserved lemons	Caramel sauce

in the cupboards

Pasta: rigatoni,	Chickpeas	Enchilada sauce
angel hair, linguine,	Fermented	Canned green chilies
spaghetti, tagliatelle	black beans	Callebaut chocolate
Rice: basmati, arborio,	Artichoke hearts	Sea salt and dark
sushi, wild and	Maple syrup	chocolate bars
brown rice	Honey	Stock: chicken, beef
Grain: quinoa, farro,	Olive oil	and vegetable
couscous	Vinegar: balsamic,	Maldon sea salt
Cornmeal	rice wine, red wine	Za'atar
Panko	Soy sauce	Sumac
Canned tuna	Coconut milk	Red chili flakes
Sardines	Canned tomato filets	Dried spices (including
Oysters	Tomato paste	many Indian spices)

"Together again."

WHITEWATER COOKS

together again